Fragments

Fragments

Linda R. Anderson

To order additional copies of this book, contact:
Xlibris Corporation
1-888-795-4274
www.Xlibris.com
Orders@Xlibris.com
62526

Contents

DEDICATION

This book is dedicated to my amazing mother, Lucy Mae Anderson, whose life was a gift to her children. Our home was filled with laughter and love, and you fed us joy daily! You were nothing short of wonderful! Oh how I adored you. Your flame still burns in my heart. Thank you for the fragments! I can't wait for Brooke to meet her grandmother in heaven!

In memory of Sylvia . . .

Yours was one of the most creative minds I've ever enjoyed. Yours were the most loving, nurturing, and comforting hands I've ever felt, next to our mother's. Your laugh was contagious and made me forget my troubles. Your advice was sound. Your voice, soulful and warm. Your presence, captivating. Your brilliance, blinding. Your kindness and generosity, immeasurable. Your sense of humor kept us in stitches . . . appropriately so, you were a nurse. Your example as a mother, wife, daughter, sister, aunt, and friend was perfection. Your love . . . amazing. Thank you for being my inspiration on so many levels. You wore grace, forgiveness, acceptance, strength, compassion, and love like a garment. I will wear your hand-me-downs proudly. I miss you.

In memory of Lucy Ann and Bob...

You both left us much too soon. Lucy, you were our mother's namesake. A sweeter, gentler soul could never be found. Bobby, your laughter continues to echo through the corridors of our lives. Your guitar playing will resume in the heavenly band for which you auditioned on earth.

Acknowledgements

First, to my godly father, precious Daddy, your words have brought us so much joy and wisdom through the years, and you have given me so much to write about! You have been faithful and steadfast. You loved our mother wholeheartedly, teaching us the meaning of possibility. Thank you, Dad! To my wonderful siblings, Al (strong and kind—king of the belly laugh), Gil (singing preacher, ministry mentor, and friend), Lucy-Ann (gentle baby), Bobby (funny man with gifted hands), Syl (sweet, singing angel), Julie (affectionate poet), Nette (Mini-Mom and nurturer), and Mike (Baybro, the brilliant minded comedian), growing up as one of 9 children showed me the virtue of loving, the value of laughter, and the blessing of sharing. I'm thrilled most to have shared a life with you! With each of your magnificent personalities and strong qualities, I have been influenced favorably. I love you all uniquely and completely. And to my Brookie, I don't know what I was doing before you came into my life. You are the joy additive that has sweetened my days perfectly. I love you, my beautiful, funny girl! The all-time texting champion of the world, maybe you'll be the next writer in the family. To the rest of my family, aunts and uncles, nieces and nephews, greats and cousins, and my godmother, Miss T, I'm so grateful to share the familial fabric with all of you. We make a lovely quilt! To my girls, whom I love, L&L&G-Nope, you have blessed me with so much love and support through the years . . . over 30! Lisa, you said I could. Loretta, you said I should. Gina, you said I would. The three of you provided me with motivation during times when I didn't want to move. Your loving push also had lift. Thank you! To my prayer partner Suzie-Q, you rock! You backed me and blessed me immeasurably, and held my hands up! I can't thank you enough! Pastor Hobdy (Cleve), you've been my spiritual guide throughout this process. Many thanks to you! To Hallerin, thank you for your suggestive therapy, making me believe that anything is possible. Vicki, you cheered me on in the home stretch! Thank you! To my together godsis, you're next, Kris. Rog—your music was often my work soundtrack. And to all who have prayed for me, encouraged me, and asked me when I would "write it down", thank you for fanning the flame of accomplishment for me. I praise God for you!

Gather up the Fragments

When they were filled, he said unto his disciples, Gather up the fragments that remain, that nothing be lost. John 6:12

We spend so much of our lives hastily rushing through experiences without taking the time to fully appreciate them or construct vivid memories of important events. Such was the case for the disciples of Jesus during His time on earth. In fact they were so sidetracked by the excitement that many of them missed out on the real significance of this incredible privilege. As a result, when the dark clouds that would signify the end of their time with Christ hovered over, casting long shadows over their joy, they faltered. This, even after having been given an up close and personal account of the power of the man, Jesus, and having been taught first hand by the Son of God. In this familiar story of the feeding of the multitude, more than one miracle takes place. Certainly it's impressive that Jesus was able to take a little sack lunch from a boy and turn it into a buffet to marvel any modern day family style restaurant. But having grown up in a family of 9 children, I watched my mother perform similar miracles with what was in our cabinets at the end of the week. Another miracle is that there was no stampede and no riots broke out over whose piece of fish or barley cake was bigger. I'm also awed by the fact that in the end, there remained 12 baskets of leftovers. But Jesus' words are what stand out most in my mind. He told the disciples to "gather up the fragments that nothing be lost." The disciples, although they had been with Him for 3 years, missed what He was saying altogether. They thought Jesus was instructing them to get out the Ziploc bags and make sure none of the leftovers went to waste. Had they understood, they would have known that he wasn't just referring to the food, but he was giving them a deeper and more pertinent lesson. What he was telling them they needed to do was store up the power of this experience and the richness of the moment. He wanted them to gather up encouragement in this hour for the hour to come. They didn't get it. Consequently, when the hour of persecution and ultimately Christ's crucifixion occurred, they cowered and fled. All of the years of wonder-working power, which they had both witnessed and performed, evaporated into panic, denial and even betrayal. They despaired. They hadn't gathered up the fragments of hope and strength that Christ had provided. Thus when the days grew dark, they were destitute of the necessary power that they were to have stored—gathered up. I have taken a lesson from them. I now seek to gather up the fragments of every good experience so that when dark days come, and they will, I will be able to draw on the joys of yesterday to carry me through today and tomorrow. During family visits and time with my Dad, I listen to every story and gather up the fragments of laughter and joy. I watched my daughter sleep as a baby and gathered up the fragments of those tender moments. When I am with friends, I am gathering up fragments so that if the day should come when those joyous times are no more, I will be able to feast on the memories and be full. My mother passed away in 1992 at the end of a vacation week in my home in Baton Rouge, LA. That week I didn't realize it but I was gathering up fragments. The stories she told me, the meals she prepared for me, the laughter, the foot massages I gave her . . . they were all fragments. Now when I am desperately lonely for that dear, sweet woman whose hands combed my hair, bandaged my knees, and cupped my face on my wedding day, I have those fragments to carry me through. Several months after my mother's death, Ruth Muse, a close and dear friend of hers and our family, invited us to dinner at her home in CT. She told us she had something special for us. While we were seated at her lovely dining room table, she disappeared into the kitchen and returned with a piping hot dish. She set it on the table before us and announced that it was a pan of lasagna that my mother had made for her just before she took the trip to my Baton Rouge home. When this precious woman learned of my mother's death, she immediately froze it so that she could serve it to us one day. We sat in tearful silence and joy . . . then we dug in! I cannot adequately describe for you just how delicious those fragments were. But I can tell you that the experience was yet another fragment. Like Jesus, I want to urge you to gather up fragments in your life that will sustain you in the future. Slow down and take note. Drink in and relish. If you gather up enough hope and joy, they can counteract sorrow and pain or at least make them more palatable. Gather up the fragments, my friend . . . so that nothing is lost. *These things have I spoken unto you, that my joy might remain in you, and that your joy might be full. John 15:11*

So

Let the redeemed of the Lord say so . . . Psalm 107:2

Conveyed in this text is a very simple instruction. If you know that you have been redeemed, or rescued from something or someone, you need to say something! The Psalmist suggests that if God has done something for you, you need to open up your mouth and say so. I am in full agreement. There is power in a testimony. Yet, in my life, I have discovered another connotation or spin, if you will, on this text. My translation . . . the LAV (Linda Anderson Version) implies that if you know that the Lord has done something for you, when presented with what appears to be a set of insurmountable obstacles, you need to be able to say, "so." This requires taking the "chosen response". You see, you may not be able to control the *action*, but you can definitely control the *reaction*. As a child, one of the most successful ways of shutting down other kids who would tease or ridicule you was to respond to their rudeness with the word, "so." It was also quite annoying to the would-be bully or teaser. "I'm not going to be your friend anymore!" Response, "So." "You don't live in a nice neighborhood." Response, "So." "We're having a party and you're not invited." By now, you should know the proper response . . . "So." In my adulthood, I've learned to give the same response to things beyond my control; malicious treatment inflicted on me by others; and the sometimes ridiculous commentary which people with way too much time on their hands feel it necessary to utter concerning me. Let the redeemed of the Lord say so, whom He hath redeemed from the hand of the enemy. I am a longtime believer that the Christian reaction to situations should be vastly different than that of the non-believer. We believe in God and we are aware of His mighty power to save, so that gives us the edge.

It doesn't mean that we won't suffer or experience dark times and hardships, get hurt or angry or experience disgust, but what it does mean is that we will respond differently. Or we should. The reaction by the child of God should not be the same as that of those who don't know Christ. The Divine Knowledge starter pack that each Christian is given should contain faith, sense, and self-control. And when presented with distasteful circumstances, the response should be a controlled response. (*Ephesians 4:26—Be angry but sin not.*) Anger should never rule you. Learn to say "so." People's opinions of you should never define you. Learn to say "so". So . . . what a powerful little word. Still asking "How so?" Well, when used in the context in which I have just shared, it conveys the thought that the redeemed don't really have to worry over foolishness. God has already snatched you from the hand of the enemy. You are redeemed . . . say "so."

A Light in Dark Places

The light shines in the darkness, and the darkness can never extinguish it. John 1:5

I have a junk drawer in my kitchen. It didn't start out as a junk drawer; it was a place to store odds-n-ends. But over time it became the drop zone for any and everything, and now it's a junk drawer. Things like scissors and small screwdrivers, pencils, shish kabob skewers, tape, and items you occasionally need that fall under the heading of etcetera, you name it, they are all in that drawer. Put a bookmark here. You'll find one of those in my junk drawer, which I'll get back to. God often gives encouragement in unmistakable ways. You just have to be paying attention. When I'm alert and paying attention, His messages come through clearly, as if someone turned on a light. Such was the case a few mornings ago when I was up in the early hours, preparing a large dinner for friends. Feeling a little less than chipper and cheery, I really would have preferred to be sleeping so as to drown out the chaos of my week. But the dinner wasn't going to make itself, so there I stood, stirring, garnishing, basting, mixing, chopping, and performing every other culinary exercise that would bring me closer to having happy, full dinner guests. Speaking of full, this day already seemed too full. In fact, life seemed cluttered for me. Have you ever felt full and empty at the same time? Well, that's just how I felt. Later that day I would have a house filled with guests, but in that quiet moment, with my family sleeping soundly upstairs, I felt so totally alone in the dark. Life that week had been drudgery and I felt dumped on. I was tired, no, more like weary and overwhelmed. For me, this was a dark moment. Back to the bookmark . . . As I prepared one of the main dishes, it required toothpicks so I went to my cluttered junk drawer for them and when I opened it, to my surprise the flashlight in the drawer was turned on. I have no idea how it happened, but the light was on in the closed, dark, cluttered drawer. The moment I saw this, it was as if a light went on in my spirit. And I got the message. "I know it's dark right now and you feel like your life is in the same condition as this junk drawer, but I'm here, and my light is still shining." That message of encouragement came straight from God to me. And the area of the drawer where the light was shining was warm. Where God shines in our lives, He makes it warm. Amid the clutter, the tape, the scissors and toothpicks of life, God's light is still shining. Feel its warmth and be encouraged, just as I was. God wants to make His presence known to us in our darkest of times. We just have to be paying attention and looking for the light. *Wherefore he saith, Awake thou that sleepest, and arise from the dead, and Christ shall give thee light (Ephesians 5:14).* The light He gives brings understanding, hope, direction, fulfillment, and it shines through the clutter. What a beautiful reminder of that fact I received that morning. And dinner was delicious.

First Things First

Trust in the Lord with all thine heart and lean not to thine own understanding. In all thy ways acknowledge Him and He shall direct thy path. Proverbs 3:5

My brother came to my bedroom door just as I was about to go to sleep and gave me the unwelcome news, "Something's wrong with the stove." I heaved a sigh of disgust and worry, muttering, "It's always something." Right away I thought all the way to the worst-case scenario. I would have to buy a new stove. This was certainly not on my list of things to do, not in the budget, and not the kind of shopping that I was looking forward to. Shoes? Yes. A stove? No. I dragged myself out of bed and walked the plank downstairs to see what I was dealing with. For some reason, the surface light wouldn't go off. My brother and I tried to assess the problem. We traded ideas, "Maybe it's a short in the wiring." "Maybe the surface of the stove is still hot from when I cooked dinner earlier. But that was hours ago and the stove should be cool by now." My mechanical expertise then suggested that I take my trouble-shooting a step further. The light bulb went off, so to speak, and I had an idea. "I'll unplug it!" Sheer brilliance. "Perhaps unplugging it for a while and then plugging it back in will reset it." My scientific partner agreed. I dragged the stove out of its tight spot between two counters, climbed behind the stove and yanked the huge plug out of the socket. I felt smart. While we had the stove away from the wall, we decided to sweep and clean all the debris that accumulates behind your stove. We scrubbed the walls and sides of the stove and then remembered our original mission. With a drum roll, we plugged the stove back in to see if the light had gone off. To our disappointment, the red light still burned brightly. Our self-applause stopped abruptly.

It was late, we were tired, and we had failed in our efforts. We were now resigned to the fact that we would have to bite the bullet and call a real repairman, and perhaps, ultimately, purchase a new stove. I wiggled the stove back into its place with another heavy sigh and stared at the stove in frustration. Just then I noticed something. One of the knobs was not turned completely off. With a click, I turned it a fraction to the left and out went the light. My brother and I looked at each other in stupefied silence. We felt like Dumb and Dumber. All that work and tussling with a heavy stove. All that worry over the possibility of having to buy a new one. Why hadn't we checked the knobs first? Okay, spiritual application time. How often do we go the long way, arrive at the worst-case scenario, take unnecessary steps and sigh in disgust before we pray? Prayer, like checking the knobs, should be the first course of action. Prayer not only can open your mind to other possibilities, more importantly, it opens heaven and a wealth of help from on high. The next time you are presented with a problem, before you rely on your own expertise and trouble-shooting strategies, first things first—pray. What a novel idea, isn't it? I'm not trying to over-simplify problems, but how often do we over-complicate them? Why not pray before we act, to invite God's involvement in our attempts to find a solution? Now if your problem is a medical emergency, I would encourage you to pray as you seek medical attention. And if you are in danger, pray while you're dialing 911. But, by all means, make prayer your initial response to the problem. That's the advice from the Original Expert . . . He suggests that, "Men ought always to pray, and not to faint." (Luke 18:1) In other words, don't fail to pray, Einstein. It's the best idea you can come up with.

Holding Patterns

They that wait upon the Lord shall renew their strength. They shall mount up on wings as eagles. They shall run and not be weary, they shall walk and not faint. Isaiah 40:31

Before you begin reading this, I want you to just say the word "wait." It was the last leg of my flight from Seattle to Atlanta. I had been flying all day long and was fatigued, exhausted, and eager to get there. Just as our flight was about to make its final approach, the pilot came on the intercom and announced that we would be delayed. He said that there was bad weather in Atlanta and it wasn't safe to land there just yet, so we would have to assume a "holding pattern." Instead of arriving at our scheduled time, we would be getting there about 20 to 25 minutes late. I groaned and twisted in my seat like an impatient child. I was due to speak at a local church in a little over an hour and knew I would be pushing it to get to the church on time even without the delay. This would really interfere with my plans. He further announced that sometimes these delayed estimated times of arrival sound more pessimistic than they really are and we might actually wind up being almost on schedule, but he didn't want to make any promises. So, for now, we were in this holding pattern over Rome, Georgia. We would have to wait until the weather improved enough for a safe landing. I wanted to get to my destination, but I was being forced to wait. I had no idea how long. Well, before I knew it, the pilot was again on the intercom. This time his announcement was far more optimistic. "Ladies and gentlemen, this is your captain. The bad weather over Atlanta has lifted and it looks like we might actually get in pretty close to our scheduled time." I cheered in my spirit. The holding pattern was over.

The wait didn't kill me and I got where I was going safely. It occurs to me that in our lives, God may have us in a "holding pattern." Our business venture isn't taking off as quickly as we'd like, we're desperate to meet Mr. or Miss Right, maybe we're trying to get our ministry off the ground and it's taking what seems like forever, we want to settle down and have a family but it's not happening. Perhaps God has you in a holding pattern because where you are trying to get isn't safe yet. There are times when God says, "yes." Sometimes He says, "no." But sometimes He says, "wait." Waiting requires trust. We have to trust that the One who has us waiting, has us waiting for "SOMETHING." We're not waiting in vain. He just has us in a holding pattern while He prepares what He has in store for us. Don't get impatient. Don't panic. Wait. When the place you're trying to get to is safe, He'll allow you to land there. In the meantime, enjoy the holding pattern and envision His arms wrapped around you, "holding" you securely until you're ready for your blessing and it's ready for you. Wait.

Too Heavy to Carry

And they came unto the brook of Eshcol, and cut down from thence a branch with one cluster of grapes, and they bare it between two upon a staff . . . Numbers 13:23

When you read the title of today's thought, did your mind automatically focus on burdens or cares, the weight of which is sometimes too much? The nature of life in a cumbersome world might make one prone to think that something being too heavy to carry would likely be less than favorable. I want you to rethink the idea, however. Sometimes there are blessings that come our way, which, without the correct attitude, may be too heavy for us. Go with me to Israel. Moses sends in a group of men to scope out the land and come back with a report. There, these spies find grapes that are so large that they can hardly carry them. They have to place the cluster on a staff and carry it between two men. The land is overflowing with milk and honey and is ideal for these wandering and weary travelers, searching for a home. You may already know the rest of the story. Along with the monster grapes, the earlier scouts brought back a false report that it would be impossible to possess the land or obtain the blessings waiting there. A visionary named Caleb then took one look at the blessings and said, "This land has our name written all over it. This blessing is for us!" And there you have it. An example of how perspective can determine whether your blessings can be too heavy for you to carry. You see, the blessings of God often come with a need for strength enough to handle them. They can be so bountiful and huge that it takes a special person to manage them. And, like some burdens, some blessings aren't meant to be carried alone. God desires to bless us abundantly. He has a thousand ways to bless us that we don't have a clue about. And some of the things he has in store for us are larger than we can even imagine. Like the grapes that had to be carried on a staff between two men. We have to be up to the task of accepting and carrying the blessing. Blessings have responsibilities. Are you up for the challenge of bearing the weight of the things that God has designed for you? The wonderful thing about the Designer is that when He provides the blessings for you, He will also equip you with the qualities necessary to handle them. Whether or not you elect to utilize the blessing management equipment is another matter entirely. God merely makes it available to you, knowing that if you fail to use it you may also fail to see the full benefit of the blessing. So, your mission in scoping out the blessing is simple. See what God has for you as yours, accept the responsibility of it and carry it with dignity. It may require enlisting the help of someone else to aid you in supporting the weight of what God has bestowed upon you. Some blessings are meant to be shared.

Do-it-Yourself Humility

Humble yourselves in the sight of the Lord, and he shall lift you up. James 4:10

Growing up in church, we would often participate in an afternoon program known as MV, which stood for Missionary Volunteers. It was an activity that we looked forward to because it involved plays and Bible games and singing and just plain old fun. One of the songs we often sang was called "Humble Me," and it was a favorite because of its clever and comical verses that referenced the journey toward heaven in satirical lyrics. For example, one verse said, "You can't get to heaven on roller skates, because you'll roll right past those pearly gates." Somewhat corny, yes, but humorous, nonetheless. Each verse brought with it laughter. As I grew older, I began to take the message in the song more seriously and would often ask God to humble me so that I could do His will. I recognized that there were aspects of my life where a good dose of humility would be useful. After preaching what I believed to be a thought-provoking message in a New England church one Saturday, I customarily stood at the door of the sanctuary to greet members of the congregation as they departed. Many offered complimentary remarks about the sermon and expressed appreciation for what I had shared. I graciously thanked each and redirected the glory to God. As the line drew toward the end, a gentleman came to me and extended his hand to shake mine. But instead of offering words of praise and appreciation he gave me a message all his own. "You stated in your sermon that we need to ask God to humble us, but I don't agree with that." Struggling to keep the smile on my face intact and show no signs of my shock and embarrassment, I thanked him for his observations. He continued, "It's better if we humble ourselves . . . like the Bible says." Immediately my mind took me to one of my favorite texts, which I somehow omitted from the manuscript of what I thought was an impactful message. "Humble yourselves in the sight of the Lord and He will lift you up." In that moment his statement gained credibility and his point was proven. On that day, the Lord humbled me, just as I had been asking. It certainly would have been a more comfortable thing for me to have humbled myself, but God had obliged me. All of the accolades and encouraging statements from the previous greeters seemed to vanish into non-existence as I stood there in the doorway of that church with this gentleman. It became the entryway to humility. I thanked him, we embraced, he left and I continued greeting the last few individuals who waited to talk to this humble speaker. I can't tell you what any of them said, but what that one soul who dared to give me counsel said remains in my mind to this day. I have found truth in his admonition. For throughout the Bible there are instances where God had to humble individuals who would not take steps to do so themselves. Saul was humbled on the road to Damascus en route to becoming Paul. Blindness then poor eyesight were the residuals of that humbling. God humbled Moses for smiting the rock that he was merely supposed to speak to. Bet it would have been nice to enter the Promised Land along with the other Children of Israel, even if they did get on his nerves. Nebuchadnezzar was humbled . . . wound up needing a manicure and a shower in the worst way. And the list goes on. God resisteth the proud but gives grace to the humble. *(Verse 6)* And it really is best that we humble ourselves rather than make our Father have to "come up those stairs," so to speak. Certainly we can ask God to help us have a change of heart. But we would be wise to make an effort to humble ourselves before Him and avoid the harsher form of behavior modification. By the way, I still like the song, but only for its entertainment value.

Binoculars

For our conversation is in heaven; from whence also we look for the Savior, the Lord Jesus Christ.

Philippians 3:20

It's amazing how binoculars can bring far away objects so close, optically, that you'd think you could almost touch them. They are basically telescopes mounted side by side to allow the viewer to use both eyes to see things at a great distance. With these magnifying glasses of sorts, you can see clearly what, with the naked or natural eye might appear as nothing more than a microscopic blip on the visual radar. Binoculars are used by outdoorsmen to see mountain crests and peaks to which they're hiking. They are used in concert halls, opera houses and theatres, allowing those seated in the nosebleed section to view the performers so closely and clearly that they could almost see the freckles on their faces. Binoculars transform what look like ants into people, dots into cars, and other fuzzy, out of focus images into what you'd realize they are if you could actually see them up close. "No, that's not a smudge, it's a house." Binoculars bring the far away to within your grasp. There's a delightful restaurant in West Seattle, Washington called Salty's. It's situated comfortably on the waterfront of Alki Beach and has a breathtaking view of the Seattle skyline and the Puget Sound. I've been a guest of that particular restaurant more times than I care to admit, and have enjoyed the view with sailboats, ferries and other vessels moving gently by, seagulls flying and sea lions occasionally making an appearance. The entire restaurant is encased in windows so that the scenery can be taken in fully. The food is great too. Okay, end of commercial. But on my last visit, I was able to take my eyes off my crepes and Belgian waffles long enough to notice that the restaurateurs have placed binoculars in receptacles throughout the dining area. Obviously they are aware of how nice it might be for guests to be able to see the city more closely. The distant view is beautiful . . . absolutely breathtaking, but with the binoculars the distant city is brought into focus and its intricacies made more vivid. The beauty of the sailing vessels and cruise ships in the Seattle docks isn't so far away. Maybe that's what we need in our spiritual lives. Spiritual binoculars that will allow us to see the distant city . . . that would be heaven . . . more closely. With our dual telescopes, we could see with both eyes the intricacies of what God is preparing for us, and it wouldn't seem so far away. We'd almost feel as if we could touch it. If we could see heaven more closely, then we could lay claim to it in a more tangible way. And if heaven were closer, we might not be so inclined to get sidetracked by the immediate objects of life. If we could look through our spiritual binoculars we'd see the healing, the hope, the help that seems so distant . . . so far away. Well, God's promise is just that pair of binoculars that we need. He has promised that in just a little while, He that shall come will come and will not tarry. (Hebrews 10:37) So right now although we may see through a glass darkly, soon God will bring everything into focus. For now, simply turn your eyes upon Jesus and look full in His wonderful face . . . then the things of earth will grow strangely dim in the light of His glory and grace.

And The Winner Is ...

I have fought a good fight, I have finished my course, I have kept the faith: [8] *Henceforth there is laid up for me a crown of righteousness, which the Lord, the righteous judge, shall give me at that day: and not to me only, but unto all them also that love his appearing.*
2 Timothy 4:7-8

Human beings, it seems, are so fixated on winning. We have so many forms of competition with winning being the goal of each. Advertisers hold contests aimed at drawing interest in a product by appealing to our lust for winning. Professional sports generate billions of dollars pitting one team against another with fans of each completely absorbed in the game to see if their team will win. Our children are involved in amateur team sports and parents have been known to obsess over their child's winning status to the point that they come fist to cuffs with other parents. There are Pie Eating contests, which I think I could win, and Olympic events, which I'm certain I couldn't. We have Spelling Bees, pageants, Oscars, Tony Awards, Emmys, Grammy Awards, and even Tractor Pull competitions. One year Richard Penniman, better known as Little Richard, was a presenter at the Grammys. When the time came for him to open the envelope and call the name of the winner, he unfolded the secret ballot and as suspense mounted he announced, "And the winner is . . . ME!" The crowd laughed, especially since Little Richard wasn't even one of the nominees. But then he persisted with the joke to the dismay of the audience, repeating several more times, "And the winner is . . . ME!" He finally announced the real winner, but his performance revealed his true desire to be a winner. We thrive on competition and winning. And even our country's governmental system is based on the elective process where votes are cast and the one garnering the most votes wins. Candidates run expensive campaigns in hopes of winning. No one wants to be the loser. Everyone wants to win. Winning is the brass ring. Tonight I watched television coverage of several elections across the nation. Some of the races were close, others landslide victories. In each someone went home defeated. It gave me pause to think about how Jesus might fare in some of the elections of today. The last time he was on earth, he lost an election. The crowd called, "Give us Barabbas!" But then Jesus showed himself to be the true winner as He ascended to heaven to sit at the right hand of the Father. While He certainly has the vote of every true Christian, there remain others who do not agree with His policies and who don't support His initiatives. He is not the winner in or of their hearts. While we as humans place so much importance on winning, Jesus isn't trying to win a popularity contest with us. You see He's already won and now He wants to see to it that *we* come out winners. And not of some temporal prize, but He wants us to win something of eternal value. He wants us to finish the course and keep the faith so that we might obtain the prize set aside for winners. And the good news is everyone can win. We are not competing against each other. The only one we're competing against is Satan, and God has already given us the victory over Him if we accept it. Because of His victory, we all get to go home winners.

His Eye Really is on Sparrows ... Hummingbirds Too

It is good that a man should both hope and quietly wait for the salvation of the Lord.

Lamentations 3:26

Have you ever encountered a situation in which you felt powerless? And even though you knew the matter was out of your hands, you felt as if you just had to do something. Several years ago I was in just that situation. A relative of mine was about to make a decision that I was sure would mean ruin. And being the knowledgeable and wise person that I am, who has never made a mistake, I thought it was my job to rescue this person. Not exactly. To the contrary, because I had made similar blunders I didn't want to see this person experience the pain I had, in my own foolish folly. Coming out of one family tragedy, I feared we were about to experience another. I had prayed and agonized with this individual, yet the person remained determined to proceed along the course, which I was certain would end in destruction. That day, as I drove to the radio station where I worked, I lamented and cried in my car, presenting what I thought was a compelling argument to God for why He needed to intervene and do something immediate and drastic. As I tearfully recited my list of concerns, I heard a voice in my head . . . almost audible. In stern tones it asked, "How dare you think that you love him more than I do?" The rebuke silenced me. When I could speak again, "I'm sorry, God." was the only intelligible thing I could utter. Though repentant, my sorrow continued. Throughout my radio program I offered Biblical passages and inspirational thoughts that seemed tailor made for me. Little did my listeners know, that the one behind the microphone offering flowery words of encouragement needed some herself. The moment I would start the next song, I would stretch out on my face, prostrate before God, on the floor of the studio and pour out my agonies for this loved one. Although I had been given a chilling reminder back in the car, that God cared and had a plan, I still wore my sackcloth and ashes and lamented at the gate for this relative. During my three-hour program, somewhere between the high praise, the Bible passages, and the Toyota commercials, I settled down. I had accepted the fact that God had my loved one in His sights and I could relax and let him handle the matter of salvation. What I had been preaching over the airwaves about the power of God's love had reached ME. With swollen eyes and a red nose, I may not have looked like I felt better, but I did. As I left the station and headed to my car along the cobblestone walkway, admiring the lovely, Connecticut foliage, I noticed a bright green leaf on the ground. In fact I nearly stepped on it but followed the odd impression in my heart to step around it. This prompting made me curious, so I bent down to see why this leaf was so special. Just then I realized that it wasn't a leaf after-all, but a tiny hummingbird, its foot stuck in the crack between the cobblestones. I gave it a nudge with my finger and up it flew. Startled, I stood up quickly and the little bird hovered in front of my face for a moment as if to say, "Thank you for freeing me." God had given me one last reminder that He takes care of us. He must have known how forgetful I tend to be. So he gave me a practical lesson in God Cares 101. I thought of the text found in Luke 12:6 -7, "Are not five sparrows sold for two pennies? And not one of them is forgotten before God. Why, even the hairs of your head are all numbered. Fear not; you are of more value than many sparrows." If God cared about a hummingbird stuck in a crack and about to become lunch for some hungry, stray cat, how much more does He care for us, His children? That's why He says, "Leave it to me." You may not understand His method of handling a situation, but His ways are past finding out. (Romans 11:33) Whatever it is that you are lamenting about right now in your life, I guarantee God is fully aware of the situation and He has the power to handle it in His way and in His time. Relax and let Him be God.

Dividing Lines

Behold, how good and how pleasant it is for brethren to dwell together in unity. Psalm 133:1

Do your words sever and cause division or do they unite? The talk phenomenon is a growing one. Talk show hosts increase in popularity and notoriety. I have long been a fan of talk radio, having once been a part of it. Their lines are sometimes rehearsed and polished, but they often speak off the cuff with ideas and views that are heartfelt and impassioned. They evoke a range of emotion and prompt us to think. Hearing the observations and philosophies of others is something that I find fascinating. Talk show personalities command a great deal of authority and even wield power. And this is true whether or not their views are mainstream. In fact, it is becoming an ever increasing trend for those who are the most outlandish and even absurd to be among the most revered and celebrated. Corporate America has realized the power of words and has seized upon this form of expression as a commodity. Even the world is aware of how powerful the tongue actually is. So what are we saying with this powerful device? Are we using it to heal or hurt . . . to mend or menace? And the words that we say, our 'lines' if you will, do they divide or bring together people of divergent backgrounds? So much of what's said today is aimed at separating and forming sides. They amount to nothing more than grievous words that stir up anger. I want the words of my mouth and the meditation of my heart to be acceptable to God and palatable to man. I want to speak words that heal and encourage. I want to use my speech to soothe and uplift. The tongue is a powerful thing. Sadly, many have taken the right of free speech to an unhealthy extreme and used that power to tear down and tear apart. Imagine the peace and sense of connectedness that could be enjoyed if our lines, the words we speak, were chosen more carefully and kindly. Before you open your mouth, contemplate the impact of the words you will speak. When I was a child my mother used to tell me to "think before you speak." I wish I could say that I have followed that instruction consistently. There are certainly words that I wish I could have sucked back in like spaghetti. But if we could all take that advice to heart and make peace our language perhaps there wouldn't be so many dividing lines. Out of the abundance of the heart, the mouth speaketh (Luke 6:45). So, the key is to let your heart be filled with love and compassion. Then what spills out of the heart, through the mouth, might build up and not tear down. *Let no corrupt communication proceed out of your mouth, but that which is good to the use of edifying, that it may minister grace unto the hearers (Ephesians 4:29).*

Noise Reduction

Obey my voice, and I will be your God, and ye shall be my people: and walk ye in all the ways that I have commanded you, that it may be well unto you. Jeremiah 7:23

Recently, I entered the 21st Century . . . the age of technology, and traded in my portable CD player for an Mp3 player. Having grown weary of lugging around, and losing, bulky CD (imagine calling CDs bulky when I was raised in the 8-track generation) cases filled with my favorite music, I was delighted by the convenience of having thousands of songs on one handy little device. I was especially thrilled to carry along my new gadget on flights. But on my first such trip, to my dismay, I couldn't hear a solitary note because I didn't have the right headphones. All of that beautiful music and no way of hearing it because of the aircraft noise. What a long flight that made for with no music. What I would have given for just one CD. I then learned that what I needed was a set of "noise reduction" headphones. As soon as I reached my destination, I rushed to the store and picked up a pair. This battery-powered headset had a switch that once activated drowns out all outside sounds and enhances the sound playing through the headphones. This allows you to hear the music clearly, free of outside noise. In fact, while the noise reduction feature is engaged, even if someone is yelling or other sounds are blaring, you can only barely hear these outside noises, if at all. So the soothing, desired sound of music is made more audible, while the unwanted clamor is eliminated. If only we could acquire such a spiritual device. One that would allow the user to drown out the clamor and noise of the enemy and his agents while making clearer and more audible the soothing and desired sound of God's voice. So often the noise of the world distracts and disturbs us. It prevents us from hearing clearly the sweet heavenly sounds sent by the One Who wants to console and encourage, comfort and cheer us . . . the One who wants to give us instruction so that all may be well with us. Instead we hear the enemy's negative droning. We hear the criticism, the accusation, the foolish advice, and the condemnation he hurls at us for having followed it. If we could tune in God and tune out the noise, oh the incredible peace we could experience. Well, actually we do have a noise reduction device. It's called prayer. When activated we are able to commune with God and block out the racket. In prayer we can ask God to enable us to hone our listening skills and focus on His voice. He has such beautiful melodies of hope for us to hear if we'll seek to be in tune with Him. But this devise must be turned on . . . engaged. With regular use, we become better able to tune out and tune in. It is the devil's plot to fill our heads with so much noise that we become confused and wind up listening to his babble rather than hear what the Spirit is saying. The Spirit of the Lord is telling us we can overcome, we are loved, we are valuable, we will be victorious! The enemy is shouting we will fail, we are forsaken, we are worthless, and we should therefore give up. Flip the switch! Allow God's soothing melodies of love to be enhanced while the devil's outside noise is eliminated. It may take time and effort to reverse the effects of having listened to his clamor, but the end result will be melodious.

Juan Who?

Wherefore seeing we also are compassed about with so great a cloud of witnesses, let us lay aside every weight, and the sin which doth so easily beset us, and let us run with patience the race that is set before us. Hebrews 12:1

It was the NASCAR Busch Series in Mexico City. Yes, I was actually watching an auto race. Call me versatile. Anyway, Juan Pablo Montoya was third and favored to win. This was an especially significant race for him because it was in his homeland and such a victory for him would make history. Skillful driving and maneuvering had positioned him for a sure win. He pulled into the pit for a tire change and refueling and just then the unthinkable happened. As the service techs were filling his gas tank, the gas line broke loose. The malfunction meant there would be no way to know how much gas was being placed in the car and he may or may not have enough fuel to finish the required laps to win. A valve that cost no more than 15 cents might cost him the race. The decision was made to take another pit stop where they would attempt to repair the gas line. As the work was underway, the clock was ticking and fellow racecar drivers were moving toward snatching his victory. The repair was successful! However, as Juan Pablo Montoya re-entered the raceway, he was now 19th in a single file race. With over 20 laps to go, he could hardly get a break. Other racers jockeyed to keep him from getting ahead of them, and the possibility of Montoya winning was now slim. After having driven so well, he now might lose the race he so desperately desired to win. When asked on camera from his racecar what his thoughts were with the setbacks, and if he felt he could still win the race, he humbly stated he would simply do his best. He just kept driving and overtaking one car at a time. Lap after lap, his efforts were focused not on winning, but on overcoming. One car, then another, he was now 16th, then 15th. Commentators referred to him as a "man possessed." Montoya was praised for how he handled the turns on the track and the gains he made at each. Now down to 3rd, then 2nd, this underdog was clearly on his way to that much-desired victory, to which all races up until now had led. As he neared the last couple laps, Montoya accidentally clipped the car of his teammate. This incident put him in position to take the lead, which he did. With a tangible excitement and the cheers of the crowd, Juan Pablo Montoya took the race! In spite of his unforeseen setbacks, mechanical difficulties, and obstacles, he won the race. Now, what does a NASCAR race have to do with anything spiritual? I'm sure you're wondering. As I watched the race it was clear to me. Each of us is in our own spiritual race. There will be unforeseen setbacks and even obstacles that may put us so far back that we feel there's no earthly way we'll win this race. In fact, there *is* no earthly way. But our pit stops with God will keep us running. All of heaven is our crew, working to repair us and get us back on track. If we will stay focused, not on winning but on overcoming, we have an incredible shot at making it. And, unfortunately, we may have run-ins with teammates and other drivers as we try to make our way to the finish. But we have to keep driving. Drive skillfully and faithfully, one lap at a time. I pray that each of us will finish, with grace, this significant race and make history . . . in our eternal homeland.

What to Expect

When I was pregnant with my daughter, a close friend of mine gave me a book called, *What to Expect When You're Expecting*. I found the book to be invaluable. It gave a week-by-week, month-by-month, and play-by-play outline of what I could expect to happen during my pregnancy. It told me how the baby was developing, the changes I would experience with my body, the cause for every ache and pain, and what would happen all the way up to delivery. The book served as a comfort to me because I realized in reading it that I was not the only one to have experienced swelling, insomnia, heartburn or any of the other woeful symptoms associated with pregnancy. It also kept me advised as to the normal stages of growth my baby was undergoing. The writers of this book, having found it to be a great success, later wrote sequels such as, *What to Expect the First Year*. I read that one, as well. It too provided me with a wealth of knowledge and peace of mind. Quite naturally, a few things occurred that weren't listed in the book, but it kept me informed enough not to fret. I often wish that there were such books that we could read in our Christian walk. Books like *What to Expect When You Lose Faith*. Or, *What to Expect When Your Church Leaders Let You Down*. Here's a great one, *What to Expect When Your Loved Ones Turn Their Backs on You*. I'd definitely buy and read *What to Expect When You Make Embarrassing Mistakes*. But, there are no such books to be found at Borders or Barnes and Noble. Not technically, anyway. The Bible, however, is the best *What to Expect* book we could ever hope to find. It, in fact, outlines the details of how to cope in each of the above-mentioned situations. It may not be loaded with colorful pictures and diagrams referencing each and every ache and pain in the development process. However, it does give a play-by-play outline of what we can expect to occur in our lives as we seek the Lord and follow after righteousness. We can expect to be hated. We can expect to be persecuted. We can expect tribulation. Those are just the aches and pains. It doesn't end there, though. We can also expect to have joy unspeakable. We can expect our weeping to endure for the night and joy to come in the morning. We can expect the Comforter to come and abide with us. We can expect to find forgiveness when we ask for it. We can expect to enjoy the protection of angels who will encamp around us. And, finally, we can expect the Lord Himself to descend from heaven with a shout to come and claim us, and then we can expect to be caught up to meet the Lord in the air. The next time you are experiencing the birthing pains of Christian development and you don't know exactly what's going on, pick up the Book. You'll find all the answers in it. *Romans 15:4—For whatsoever things were written aforetime were written for our learning, that we through patience and comfort of the scriptures might have hope.*

Shortcomings

For all have sinned, and come short of the glory of God . . . Romans 3:23

Here's the scenario; you have attempted something and felt like you came up short or just missed the mark. Perhaps you have felt the uneasy sense of inadequacy that comes from believing that you just don't quite measure up. In short, you've flopped. Such insecurities are part and parcel of living in a world where perfection and excellence are the driving force. It is sometimes difficult to meet the demands of a success driven society and so feeling as if we've fallen short becomes common. And this feeling of inadequacy can cover all areas of our lives, including the spiritual. We become tempted to compare ourselves to those whom we perceive to be have achieved or those who we view as "living right" and succeeding in this Christian walk. But if we were to take a closer look at those whom we have elevated in our minds to the plateau of perfection, we might notice a wrinkle in the fabric and the halo might be a bit askew. It goes back to our key text, which simply states that nobody's perfect. Everyone has fallen short and failed to measure up at some time and in some way. It's not a comfortable feeling, but we're in good company. Prophets and kings have fallen into this same category and even the Psalmist who was known as a "man after God's own heart" was in the "less than perfect" group. So even with our shortcomings, God can do something with us . . . possibly even something great. It's our responsibility to do our best and allow God to do the rest. Stop reflecting on the sin and the falling short, and begin to focus on the redemption and standing tall. The earnest relationship with God defies the laws of gravity, which deem that what goes up must come down. With God, what goes down has the supreme opportunity to come up. We go down on our knees and come up changed to the degree that, although we have sinned and fallen short, God's grace and redeeming love can elevate us. And what God allows to go up, can stay up! When God brings us up from a low place in our lives, we don't have to wind up going down again, failing again, falling short again. In Christ, we can all measure up simply by striving to rise above. Sure, we may come short of the glory of God at times in our lives, but the mere attempt to stand tall in Him causes Him to use the measuring tape of grace. I cannot tell you the number of times I have failed, miserably. But that number is matched by the number of times God has shown me mercy and offered me a hand up. He extends to each of us that same loving lift. Whether we accept it or not is our choice. The New Testament story of Zaccheus is the perfect account of a man who did not measure up in any sense of the word. In fact he climbed up a tree to elevate himself to where he could see Christ. His actions up to that point had been despicable and certainly he fell short, but something in him compelled him to get a look at Jesus from a higher vantage point. Having come in contact with God, he accepted the lift. When Christ ordered him to come down from the tree, He, in effect, elevated him. A changed life was the result. An elevated life. That same opportunity is available even now. Shortcomings only make us aware of our need to be lifted in Jesus. When combined with the effort that we make to climb above our shortcomings, God's grace takes us beyond the limits of our past failures. Most definitely all have fallen short, but through Christ all can take it to a higher level.

Room Enough to Receive

Give, and it shall be given unto you; good measure, pressed down, and shaken together, and running over, shall men give into your bosom. For with the same measure that ye mete withal it shall be measured to you again. Luke 6:38

The concept of giving in order that we may receive is hard to fathom for many. We live in an age where so many are "in it for what they can get." Giving rarely enters the minds of many, but others are preoccupied with the thought of receiving. "How does giving make me any better off?" some might ask. The answer is found in the Instruction Manual . . . the Bible. In Malachi, God gives instructions on how we are to return to Him a faithful tithe. He simply requires that we bring back one tenth of what He has given us, as a sign of faithfulness and obedience. In return He makes a promise to us that He will open the windows of heaven and pour out a blessing to us that we simply won't have room enough to receive. Clearly, we're getting the better end of the bargain. Likewise He offers to trade us beauty for ashes, the oil of joy for sorrow, and a host of other good things in exchange for our woes . . . if we will but give them to Him. Seems kind of one-sided . . . in our favor. We give him a load of worthless junk and He gives us blessings. We give him a broken life and He gives us eternal life. In this He is attempting to show us an example of how blessed it is to give. I've been in some one-sided relationships where I was on the giving end. They left me feeling used and taken advantage of. I didn't feel appreciated or valued in any way. But God asks us to give very little and He offers to shower us with His goodness. Now of course you realize that God doesn't need our money or what we give Him, but He delights in our obedience and wants to see that we understand the merits of the equation. Once we understand the concept, we can then practice it on our fellow man, without those feelings of resentment that I mentioned earlier. We will then also experience the blessing of what He will give us in return. The Word tells us in today's text, *"Give, and it shall be given unto you; good measure, pressed down, and shaken together, and running over."*(Luke 6:38) It also informs us that it is more blessed to give than to receive (Acts 20:35). No doubt we all like to be on the receiving end from time to time, but a generous spirit inspired by God will render returns untold. I offer this admonition in the words of the older, southern folk who strongly suggested sensibility in my youth, "Baby, don't be no fool." In other words, use discernment in giving. But give where true need exists or love abounds. And, by no means am I indicating that we should give away all that we have in hopes of gaining some greater return . . . those motives would prove fruitless. But if we will give according to our hearts as led by God, He will honor what He has promised and the blessing will be measurable and often tangible. It may not come in the form of currency, but it will certainly be beneficial. In my lifetime I have been given wonderful gifts. I have been the recipient of blessings that would astonish. I firmly believe that these blessings were part grace, part love, and part reward. I certainly can't say I was deserving of them. They were 100% blessings. And whatever giving we do should by no means be done with the intent of getting something; rather it should be simply for the sake of being a blessing to someone. That intent always finds favor with God. And the giving, in and of itself, is often the reward. Like watching a person you love open a gift you have given them, which you knew would make them happy. If we give out of a sincere heart, we reflect the love of God. What greater gift could there be than that?

Greater Expectations

Now unto him that is able to do exceeding abundantly above all that we ask or think, according to the power that worketh in us.
Ephesians 3:20

There is a motto I have learned to live by that alleviates a great deal of frustration for me. It is, "Without expectation, there can be no disappointment." Yes, I'm aware it sounds a bit cynical. I'm sure you've gathered that my having adopted such a saying is indicative of the fact that I have been disappointed a time or two. You would be correct in your assessment. In life people, friends, family, associates are bound to let you down in some way, at some point and leave you feeling abandoned or stranded. Having been on the downside of that experience more times than I care to recall, I've settled upon that motto as a means of self-protection. For the most part, it has worked. I have fewer disappointments because I really wasn't expecting anything anyway. On the other hand if someone does something special, which I wasn't expecting, it's a very nice surprise. Sort of like a treat. Well, in ordinary, everyday life, with everyday people this might be an okay practice. But I thank God that with Him, I can expect something greater than I can even imagine . . . and He won't let me down. Even when my prayers are not answered in the way I mapped them out for the Lord to perform—yes, we do that, as if He needs our instructions, I still can have the expectation that He will do something greater than I imagined. He is a God Who goes above and beyond my pitiful ideas. And He desires that I shoot for the stars, dream big, anticipate the best, look for the amazing, and expect greatness. It all hinges on faith and my belief that a God Who would send His only Son to die for me certainly has every intention of enhancing the life His Son saved . . .

that being mine. Just as loving parents want the best for their children, God wants what is best for us. (*Matthew 7:11—If ye then, being evil, know how to give good gifts unto your children, how much more shall your Father which is in heaven give good things to them that ask him?*) He has greater expectations for us than we have for ourselves. When it comes to relying on people like me, I sometimes don't have the most confidence that they will come through. But as I rely on God, I have no doubt that He will come through in an amazing, mind blowing way. His love exceeds my expectations and His plans for me are bigger than anything I could concoct on even a good day. So I will look to the Lord, the Author and Finisher of my faith, with *greater* expectations . . . and I know He will not disappoint.

What are your hopes and dreams? Converse with the Father about them and ask Him to exceed your expectations in accordance with His will. His promises are true and He has said that He will do exceedingly and abundantly more than we could ask or think according to the power that is in us. Great and marvelous are Thy works, oh God . . . and thank you letting your children experience that first hand!

The Perfect Storm

And his disciples came to him, and awoke him, saying, Lord, save us: we perish. Matthew 8:25

The story is a familiar one. Jesus had spent the day preaching and was tired. He called His disciples and told them to gather in a boat and cross the water away from the crowd. What a pleasant end to a full day. Can't you see them sailing off into the sunset? The gentle rocking and swaying of the boat lulls Jesus to sleep, as the disciples look adoringly at their teacher, friend, and Savior. How precious He must have looked, sleeping so sweetly. The story should end here with Jesus relaxing and the disciples enjoying this peaceful ride with the Lord. But it doesn't. This is actually where it all starts. Soon the weather started getting rough, the tiny ship was tossed. If not for the courage of the fearless crew . . . wait, that's another story. Dark clouds begin to form and the wind changes. A once pleasant breeze now becomes more like the gale winds of a hurricane. The water gets choppy and the waves splash over the sides of the boat. Now the real story is unfolding. I don't want to focus on Jesus' ability to speak peace into the storms in your life. By now, we know that He is more than able. I don't even want to focus on Jesus' ability to sleep through what others fear. We already know that He is a fearless God of power and might. What I wish to focus on is the need for Jesus to allow storms in our lives in order to reveal to us our need for more faith. The disciples had spent considerable time with Jesus and had seen His power in many ways. They knew by now that He was the Son of God. But when the storm grew fierce and threatening, they became so afraid that they abruptly and rudely awakened the Lord out of a sound sleep. And not only that, but they awakened Him with a veiled accusation, "Master, don't you even care that we are about to perish?!" Now let's look at Who they are dealing with for a moment. This is Jesus. All-knowing and all-powerful. Do you think for one minute that He didn't know the storm was coming when He got into the boat with these characters? I have a feeling that He knew full well the weather forecast, largely because He created the world, weather, water, wind, and everything else that adds up to a storm. And I believe that knowing this storm was on its way, He decided this was the perfect time and the perfect storm to teach these men a solid lesson. Remember, time with them was scarce and He had to get in as many lessons as He could in the brief amount of time that was left. Back to the wind and waves. Jesus was sleeping through this furious storm while the disciples were bailing out water, trying to man the boat, arguing about whose fault it was that they wound up out here in this storm in the first place, trying not to lose their lunch, and choking on flying water. His ability to sleep amid all of this chaos should have given them a clue. As He slept like a baby, one or two of the disciples probably cried like babies. And, certain that their lives were about to end, they screamed, "MASTER, save us!!!" Jesus woke up with a start, and most likely annoyed, but didn't miss a beat. "Peace, be still." I often muse that Jesus was probably talking to the disciples and the wind just happened to obey too. Suddenly the storm ceased and the water was calm. I hope that Jesus rolled His eyes at this group of scared, wet men. And I hope they realized how ridiculous they appeared. Here they were in a boat with God and they panicked because of a storm. I likewise hope that we realize how ridiculous we appear when God has to allow storms in our lives so that we can learn lessons in faith. We keep praying for peace, but the lessons God is using to teach us to exercise more faith just aren't working. So He allows for the perfect storm of sickness or pain, sorrow or disappointment. If we would but learn the lesson, He would speak peace to our situation. So rather than ask for peace, perhaps we should as for faith. After all, it is the substance of things hoped for and the evidence of things not seen. You've invited Jesus into the boat of your life. He is there with you. You may think He's sleeping, but believe me He is fully aware of your storm . . . He's just resting His eyes. Trust Him to bring the storm to an end when your faith is strengthened. In the meantime, ride it out, knowing that He won't allow you to drown in your sorrows. He loves you too much to watch you perish. Begin asking God to get you to the place where you don't need storms in order to learn the lessons in faith that He wants each of us to learn.

Acquisitions

Wisdom is the principal thing; therefore get wisdom: and with all thy getting get understanding.

Proverbs 4:7

Some of the most valuable acquisitions are those which cannot be bought. Peace of mind, forgiveness, love, and wisdom top the list of those things. Society has the human race (most appropriately named) in a desperate pursuit of things, and that 'race' sometimes prevents us from gaining the most priceless of possessions. Solomon had more possessions than most could fathom. I guess you could say he was the Biblical equivalent of Bill Gates. His wealth was unsurpassed, and he had power to go with it. And all of these valuable treasures came as a result of his giving the right answer on Who Wants to be a Millionaire. God asked him what he would like if he could have any one thing, and Solomon's response was, "Give me wisdom." That was his final answer. Because he answered the question correctly, God gave him what he asked for and riches besides. Years later he would write directives for us, called Proverbs, detailing how we should live well, with wisdom being at the center of our well-being. You see, having acquired all sorts of things; wealth, homes, wives and concubines, he realized the most priceless of his "things" was the wisdom God had given him, which, by the way, he abandoned a time or two. So rather than give us a blueprint for how to get rich, he told us that in all of our gaining and getting we should try to lay claim to wisdom and understanding. The key is that he knew that should we ever get rich, so to speak, we'd need wisdom to maintain our wealth. Hence, the statement that a fool and their money are soon parted. Yes, there is a greater wealth than that which money defines. And it is accessible to even those who do not own vast amounts of land, have large bank accounts or enjoy great returns on their investments. This wealth is acquired through experience and an open mind. Knowledge makes its possessor rich. The wealthy without it are poor indeed. I could cite the names of many who would provide proof for this statement, but to do so wouldn't be wise. Suffice it to say, financial wealth alone does not make one rich. But in all of our gaining, we should seek to gain understanding or knowledge. Wisdom is the ability to act on that knowledge. When applied, we see a great return on the investment God has made in us. That car that you obtained can be totaled in a split second. The home you acquired can disappear faster than you can say the word, "foreclosure." One serious drop in the market and every sound investment you've made can hit the bottom, soundly. Knowledge and its active counterpart, wisdom, once acquired will never be repossessed, seized, lost, or confiscated. Acquire these. They are sure and secure.

Good Scars

But he was wounded for our transgressions, he was bruised for our iniquities: the chastisement of our peace was upon him; and with his stripes we are healed. Isaiah 53:5

How could scars ever be considered good? They represent pain and hurt. And they serve as a reminder of something that wounded us. Where's the good in that, some would wonder? But I know a thing or two about scars. I've had some since my childhood from bicycle accidents, falls, and other mishaps. Some, like the one over my right eye, were even caused by disobedience. I was a curious little girl. My father told me to step back as he removed a broken pane of glass from the window in our living room. I listened and stepped back, but then slyly eased forward again, without his knowledge. Paying careful attention to the large piece of broken glass that he was maneuvering, he didn't see me. As he turned, the jagged edge nicked my eyelid. It should have been worse, but where I could have been blinded, I'm merely scarred. Other scars I've acquired at various stages throughout my life resulting from clumsiness, curling iron casualties, surgeries, you name it. And no matter how much antibiotic ointment and Cocoa Butter and so-called wonder scar removal treatments I've applied, I still have them all. Most of the injuries that left these scars were self-inflicted and served no purpose. But one long, ugly scar on the inside of my left arm is pretty valuable to me. No, I'm not a sadist, but the injury was caused by love. My then 12-year old daughter stood by the stove serving herself a plate of dinner as I attempted to take a pan of bread from the oven. Like I did on that fateful day of my youth, she eased forward as I lifted the large hot pan and rather than burn her, I, instinctively, put my other, bare arm between her and the pan. Branded! I had burned myself in order to save her from being burned. Though fully healed, it sure did leave a nasty scar. But this I consider a good scar. It bears evidence of love . . . my love for my child. I may never make any effort to erase it. Wait. Who am I kidding? Vanity, at some point, will likely drive me to the nearest pharmacy for the latest brand of fade cream. But this is definitely my best scar. Jesus knows a thing or two about scars too and He has a few of His own. He acquired His for us. Seeing us about to get hurt, He put himself between us and what would have injured, destroyed, and killed us. His are good scars. They are deep scars that resulted from ugly wounds, yet the scars are beautiful. They tell of a love so incredible that I can scarce take it in. His scars heal us. I love Him for it. I don't know if my daughter even realizes the significance of the scar on my arm, even though I don't miss an opportunity to remind her, occasionally showing her the burn and asking, "See how much I LOVE you?" in my best martyr voice. But I certainly realize the sacrifice my Jesus made for me in taking the wounds meant for me. My burn helped me to understand that type love a little better. Thank you, Jesus, for the good scars.

Wings

And I said, Oh that I had wings like a dove! For then would I fly away, and be at rest. Psalm 55:6

In Greek Mythology, Icarus, the son of Daedalus was escaping from Crete on artificial wings made for him by his father. He flew too close to the sun and the wax with which his wings were fastened melted, and he fell into the Aegean Sea. How reassuring to know that we are not living mythological tales with God. It is further reassuring that the type of figurative wings our Heavenly Father has in mind for us are not artificial nor will they melt with close contact to the Son (S-O-N). One day God will give us flight and our flight training begins now in our efforts to get closer to His Son. Our reason for striving to get closer to God should not be for our own glory. If this is the case, then that pursuit will be for naught. But as we draw nearer to God, the desires of the flesh will melt away and allow the Christ in us to show through. We take on more of His characteristics and shed more of our own. The veneer of spiritual theatrics is removed and the façade of religious performance peeled off. Now, close to our Creator, we are re-made and we soar. Better than a chemical peel, this procedure has lasting, and less harmful, effects. God wants to be close to us, but we have to make the invitation and the effort to be close to Him. Once we move in His direction He begins the process of change. In His warm light, the old becomes new, hearts that would wax cold are melted and molded, and the artificial wings that look pretty yet serve no purpose are exchanged for something that will take us higher. God extends to us the opportunity to rise above our present condition and circumstances. There is lifting in Him. For the earnest Christian, we can never fly too close to the Son. There is no danger in being close to Him. In fact the closer we get, the safer we are. When we seek to be closer to God we rise above the common cares and distractions experienced at lower elevations. Being nearer to the Lord means being at rest. No melting there.

Did You Really Mean "Everything?"

In everything give thanks for this is the will of God in Christ Jesus concerning you. I Thess. 5:18

At just over 7 pounds and only 3 days old, this fragile baby girl lay naked and blindfolded in an incubator with fluorescent lights beaming down on her. Instead of being at home, tucked snuggly in her white bassinet decorated with ribbons and lace, here the baby was in the Neonatal Intensive Care Unit of a New England hospital . . . her skin and eyes as yellow as a lemon and growing more yellow by the hour. Her mother helplessly stood by watching the new baby—the restorer of her joy, her gift from God—now on the brink of being snatched away only days after she had been received. The doctors were calling it Hyperbilirubinemia. A fancy-shmancy name for acute jaundice. But this case was so severe that the infant's blood was now toxic and her life was in the balance. The baby was so weak that eating was an impossibility, yet treatment called for continual feeding and excretion as the cure. This new mom, with hopes of nursing her infant, couldn't even produce enough milk to save the baby. So now the options were to either pump all of the blood out of this tiny, weak person and replace it with donor blood or allow the doctors to place a tube down the baby's throat, through her nose, and force-feed the child back to health. Having chosen option two, she watched as this little creature, who had stolen her heart from the first cry, was "tubed" and encased in glass. The baby's heels were black and blue from all of the needle sticks to draw blood so the bilirubin levels could be checked hourly. "What is there in this to be thankful for?" she wondered. "I suppose I can be thankful for the fact that I had the opportunity to give birth," she told herself. Difficult to do with feet so swollen she couldn't wear shoes and while feeling like a gutted fish from having given birth only three days prior. "Or maybe I can be thankful for the fact that medical help is within my grasp," she said, trying harder to convince herself. But none of that seemed to take away the pain and fear of losing that precious life even before she cut one tooth, took one step or said one word. Prayers seemed unanswered thus far. With each lab result, the toxic numbers remained high. Family came to encourage the young woman and lend support. But throughout each quiet night of solitude, she watched the baby suffer. Pacing the floor, she struggled to think of positive aspects of this scenario. Finding few, she prayed on anyway, and thanked God for the desired outcome in advance. Four days later the baby was once again placed into this mother's welcoming arms. Into MY welcoming arms. Indeed, God had come through in the way in which I had prayed. He saved my little gift, Brooke, and allowed me to see her first tooth, then a mouthful . . . her first steps, then her running . . . her first words, and her back-talking that has landed her in trouble many times. I now have a visible reason to be thankful. But, what about those times when prayers are not answered in the way we hope? What about the times when circumstances don't go our way? One year earlier I watched my mother die. And, three years after Brooke's birth, I watched my 43-year-old brother placed in the ground right next to my mother. As I stood by the grave, the same words echoed through my mind that I had uttered as I stood by the incubator, looking at my baby girl for what I feared would be the last time . . . "What is there in this to be thankful for?" The answers again were few. But this one thing became clear. The thanks that we are to give to God are not circumstantial. His Word didn't tell us to give thanks only at graduations, weddings, and baptisms. We weren't instructed to be thankful during happy times with party hats, streamers, and balloons. But, "in EVERYTHING." Anyone can say thank you for good things. But the believing Christian must trust in God despite what is evident and be thankful on less than pleasant occasions. It won't all seem good, but as the young people say, "it's all good." Why? Because what God allows is up to Him. If we trust Him and believe His Word, we know that all things do work together for the good of them that love God and are called according to His purpose. We also know that our light affliction, which is but for a moment, works for us a far exceeding weight in glory. When we stop looking at the temporary as if it were eternal, we can give thanks in the midst of EVERYTHING. In trouble, thank you . . . in death, thank you . . . in sickness, thank you . . . in persecution, thank you, Jesus . . . for this is the will of God in Christ Jesus concerning you.

Due Season

And I will make them and the places round about my hill a blessing;
and I will cause the shower to come down in his season; there shall
be showers of blessing. Ezekiel 34:26

It seems most of us are waiting for this season spoken of in the above text. The season in which we will receive our promised "showers of blessing." We even sing a song in church called, "Showers of Blessings." In full harmony, we join in the chorus and ring out, "Mercy drops round us are falling . . . but for the showers we plead." We want these showers to saturate us and drench our lives. I know I do. But as I began thinking about this topic and the blessing of prosperity, health, and happiness and every other good and perfect gift that comes down from the Father of lights, I came to a startling realization. We are looking up at the sky, waiting for those blessings to fall down, but many of us aren't necessarily doing our part. You see, just as God blesses us, He expects us to be in the blessing business ourselves. Did you hear the sound of screeching tires? We are quick to ask God for things, while we often ignore our own obligation to be a blessing to others. Have you ever considered the possibility that you might be the in the weather forecast. Perhaps God intended for you to provide a little rain and share with a brother or sister who is standing in need of a blessing? And, not just those who you love or care about, but even those who have nearly caused you to forget, for a quick moment, that you are a child of God. We are admonished to "bless those who persecute you." (Romans 12:14.) And the text doesn't stop there, it instructs us to feed our enemy if he's hungry (verse 20), making no mentioning of adding poison. We need to understand that some of the inclement conditions that God allows in our lives, often brought upon us by others, are designed to reveal to God our readiness for the wonderful things He has in store for us. This is why He expects us to bless indiscriminately. You see the showers of blessings that we have the duty of pouring out are not exclusively for the people we like. God sends down rain on the just and the unjust . . . and it's a good thing because I know I've fallen into both categories at various times in my life. So as we stand with our faces to the sky and our hands lifted up as if to reach for the blessing that God has for us, let's hope that a note doesn't come floating down from the sky that reads, "And who did you bless today? Love, God." Friends, let's allow the hardships, trials, and bad weather in our lives to serve as the thunder and lightning that often precede the showers. Let us be quick to rain mercy and kindness on the lives of others and then maybe we'll be ready to receive the sweet drops from heaven that God has promised us. Isaiah 50:5 spells it out. *"The Lord has given me the tongue of the learned that I should know how to speak a work in season to him that is weary."* While we wait for God to bless us, we should be poised to bless others, in word and deed. So, now let's all sing a rousing chorus of, "Make me a blessing . . . to someone today." And then, let's turn our umbrellas upside down to catch the downpour!

When Joy is "Unspeakable"

Then he said unto them, Go your way, eat the fat, and drink the sweet, and send portions unto them for whom nothing is prepared for this day is holy unto our LORD, neither be ye sorry, for the joy of the LORD is your strength. Nehemiah 8:10

A friend and I were praying the other day, after a particularly troubling series of events. During her prayer she reminded the Lord that, "weeping may endure for a night, but joy comes in the morning." With that she added, "Okay, Lord, it's morning." I too was wondering where the much-needed joy was that that text assured me would meet me with the morning's light. I felt weak with the pressures of life and we both seemed to be feeling the crushing weight of matters beyond our control. Even after the prayer, I still felt exhausted and barely saw any light at the end of the tunnel. I recall hearing a quip once with regard to misfortune, "If I did see a light at the end of the tunnel, it would probably be an oncoming train." I was so overwhelmed that I couldn't even speak an encouraging word. I just poured out a prayer of total frustration and told God just how discouraging it all felt. My joy was indeed unspeakable, because I couldn't utter a delightful word. Well, just like that day my friend and I prayed in anguish, there will be other days and times during which we may feel like throwing in the towel (which by the way is in an ever-growing pile of unwashed laundry). Problems, sickness, issues at work, conflict with loved ones, challenges with your children, bills, a million responsibilities and the ringing phone may have pushed you to the limit and you're about to scream, "uncle . . . okay, okay, I give up!" When we reach that point . . . our end, that's when we can learn what real joy is all about. Joy is that lasting feeling that lines the bed of a river that rages out of control. It's

59

like the sun that shines above the clouds on the darkest day. You may not see it but you have to know that it's there. It's not like happiness, which is attached to something. It's just always there. We may not always feel happiness, but as believers in God's promises, we have to learn to know what joy feels like and then reach into the depths of our soul and pull it out. That feeling comes from knowing God's love and concern for you, His child, and trusting that even if your world seems way too complicated and burdensome right now, God has that world in His control. That knowledge brings with it joy. Too weak to carry all the weight of your situation? Good news, His strength is made perfect in weakness. (II Corinthians 12:9) Simply allow the joy of the Lord to be your strength. Give Him your burdens and cares in exchange for His joy. He's so loving that He's willing to make that kind of trade with you. You really can exchange a truckload of junk for lifetime worth of joy. How do I know? I'm doing it today. The Psalmist knew about this arrangement with God and wrote, *"Hear my cry O God, attend unto my prayer. From the end of the earth will I cry unto thee, when my heart is overwhelmed, lead me to the rock that is higher than I."* (Psalm 61:1-2) Today I'm piling all of my problems into the dump truck and driving it to the Rock that is higher than I. I'll unload them and drive away with twice as much joy. Why don't you do the same?

Mountains out of Molehills

And Caleb stilled the people before Moses, and said, Let us go up at once, and possess it; for we are well able to overcome it. Numbers 13:30

Mountains are an incredible wonder and such an amazing sight to behold. They can be breathtaking not just because of their beauty but because they are . . . well . . . big. I absolutely love mountains. Living in the Pacific Northwest, I have formed quite an attraction to Mt. Rainier. You could even say I'm in a love relationship with that mountain. I have even driven there a couple of times and the scenic, winding path that allows tourists to make their way up the mountain yields wonderful views. The closer you get to the mountain, however, you actually lose sight of its size. Every now and then you will catch a peek at its crest, but being on the mountain changes your perspective and makes the mountain seem not as large. And if you've ever had the opportunity to see an aerial view of a mountain, say from an airplane, for example, again these grand objects remain ominous but appear less . . . well . . . big. In our lives getting a different perspective on a seemingly gigantic object can make it less overwhelming. The huge, mountainous problem can seem smaller if you approach it and scale it. When facing life's biggest obstacles, we sometimes need to look at them from a different angle. And it might even help to ask God to give us an aerial view of the situation. From up close or above you place yourself in a more favorable position for tackling the matter, which may seem . . . well . . . big. I love "mountains". And maybe it's because each one presents me with the unique opportunity to see how God is going to help me to approach it and get over it. The mountain isn't the bad thing; in fact it's a beautiful thing of wonder. We just have to learn how to look at our mountains and how to get over them.

Add Church. Stir.

[23]Let us hold fast the profession of our faith without wavering; (for he is faithful that promised;) [24]And let us consider one another to provoke unto love and to good works: [25]Not forsaking the assembling of ourselves together, as the manner of some is; but exhorting one another: and so much the more, as ye see the day approaching.
Hebrews 10:23-25

While driving to work one day, I was having a conversation with my brother about Christian values. We talked about how there are some who profess Christianity without necessarily making any changes in their lives. He was educating me on the fact that many people, despite their profession of Christianity, still carry on lifestyles that seem contrary to Christianity. He pointed out that to call yourself a Christian, all you have to do is believe in Jesus Christ and His second coming. For many, this doesn't mean living a life that differs from that of the rest of the world, but merely going to church in addition to all of their other activities and practices. People live the same lives; they just go to church too. As if church is a magic ingredient in a bad recipe, they add it to the mix in hopes that it will make the finished product turn out well. But church, in and of itself, does not a Christian make, just as flour does not a cake make. Attending church is only one ingredient in the Christian life, and, therefore should be added to a <u>good</u> recipe. In Acts, the 16th chapter, the question was asked of Paul, "What must I do to be saved?" Paul responded, "Confess with your mouth the Lord Jesus Christ and believe that He is risen from the grave and you and your house shall be saved." In order to confess something, we must know it to be true. And true belief means acting upon that belief. I shared with my brother my view that if a person really believes in the second coming of Christ, and would appreciate experiencing that event favorably ("Lo, this is our God we have waited for Him and He will save us," not "Rocks fall on me and hide me from the face of Him that sits upon the throne"), it should spark in that person the decision to live differently than those who do not believe. That's what the Bible states, anyway. *If any man be in Christ he is a new creature. Old things are passed away; behold all things are become new (II Corinthians 5:17).* Church is a wonderful addition to the Christian life. But that life should be one that reflects Christ in so many other ways and is based on a relationship with Christ. If church is simply something we use as a signifying mark or an exercise to prove we are Christians there is a danger. What happens if someone in church injures us or if we for some reason turn away from church? Well, the only "signifying mark" of Christianity is now gone. We need more than just the ingredient of church. The rest of the recipe includes honoring God's instructions, treating our body as if it is the temple of the Holy Spirit, and showing love to one another. The rest of the Christianity recipe includes loving God and accepting His love. When combined with an already wonderful recipe, church can make our lives more complete. Church places us in fellowship with others of like faith and gives us a source of regular spiritual teaching. It also gives us a formal outlet for worship. Yet, I do not doubt that heaven will have a large delegation of Christians who rarely, if ever, made it to church. Will there be an equally large delegation of individuals who merely attended church without any real dedication to the Guest of Honor? Key to salvation is loving God and living like we love Him. Then we can add church attendance to the mix and feel more fulfilled. It will stir up our relationship with God and others who are likewise living out Christianity. A loving relationship with God and church . . . why not make this our recipe for spiritual development?

Alternate Endings

There hath no temptation taken you but such as is common to man: but God is faithful, who will not suffer you to be tempted above that ye are able; but will with the temptation also make a way to escape, that ye may be able to bear it. 1 Corinthians 10:13

One of the wonderful mysteries of heaven that I can't wait to experience is the opportunity to see how God changed the course of things in my life to save me. I long to see how things would have turned out had the Lord not intervened. And I'm excited by the thought of seeing how my guardian angel stepped in to rescue me time and time again, at God's command. How humbling to know that heaven is at full alert on our behalf. During Thanksgiving week, my pre-teen daughter wound up at the mall with one of her friends of the same age. What was supposed to be an outing with this friend and her mother turned out to be an unsupervised afternoon at the mall. I had no idea the friend's mother intended to merely drop them off. But I thank God that He knew. As they moseyed through the mall, shopping and giggling, they noticed a couple. The woman smiled at them in a seemingly friendly manner, and they smiled back. Some time later, the male of the two showed up in the Food Court where the girls where buying ice cream. He was alone this time and he approached the girls, zeroing in on my daughter. "Did you know you could be a model? You're beautiful," he told her. With that, his foot was in the door and he began to converse with her about a modeling job. She told him that her mother didn't want her talking to strangers. His response was, "Is your mother strict?" She told him that she wasn't allowed to make any decisions without her mother's permission. He continued with promises of money and clothes. This man, with clearly no good intentions, pressed my child for her name and address. After refusing several times, and now beginning to fear him, she gave him her email address. This, she hoped, would satisfy him enough to get him to leave her alone. It didn't. He persisted with his sales pitch. Finally, the friend of hers made her own cell phone ring and pretended to be talking to her mother. With this, the "devil" fled. They escaped, unscathed, but rattled. Of course when I learned of these events, I was enraged. I notified the police, the mall security, and the media. I wondered how many other unsuspecting teens had been lured by this evil person . . . and with possibly tragic results. And I was reminded of another young woman who was once fooled by the pitch of a salesman who successfully sold her on the idea of eating forbidden fruit. We are living the results of that poor choice even now. The very mall incident serves as an example of the fall-out from that error in judgment in Eden. But the outcome could have been so much worse for my daughter and her friend. And, by the devil's plan, it would have. He intended for me to be tearfully talking to the FBI on Thanksgiving, trying to ascertain whether there were any new leads on the whereabouts of my missing child. And his plan was for my daughter to be who knows where, experiencing who knows what horrors. But God provided an alternate ending! Hallelujah! In the ending God wrote, there my precious daughter sat in the den with our friends and family, Thanksgiving afternoon, eating chocolate cake and Cool Whip. Why? Because she's God's precious daughter too and He had let no harm come to her. I sighed with tired joy as I watched her, and took the last bite of my Sweet Potato Pie and ice cream. What a sweet ending. And God has provided many such endings for each of us, the half of which we do not know. When we get to heaven, we'll see what could have been. And we'll thank Him for re-writing the story of our lives.

"If you Can't Stand the Heat..."

Then Nebuchadnezzar came near to the mouth of the burning fiery furnace, and spake, and said, Shadrach, Meshach, and Abednego, ye servants of the most high God, come forth, and come hither. Then Shadrach, Meshach, and Abednego, came forth of the midst of the fire. And the princes, governors, and captains, and the king's counselors, being gathered together, saw these men, upon whose bodies the fire had no power, nor was an hair of their head singed, neither were their coats changed, nor the smell of fire had passed on them. Daniel 3:26-27

We all know well the story of the three young men of Jewish descent, who were cast into a fiery furnace because of their refusal to obey the King's command and bow down before a false God. I've always been inspired by that story because of the miraculous way in which God showed His power to all who witnessed the scene. His power to take the heat out of a fiery situation for the good of His faithful children. As I have been placed in certain fiery situations in my life, I have come to experience that power for myself. I believe that is why God allows us to endure hot trials . . . so that others can see the special effects of His deliverance. Some might wonder why God didn't rescue the boys before they had to step into a furnace that had been made seven times hotter . . . so hot, in fact that the heat killed the guards. Okay, He didn't elect to do that, so then why didn't He put the fire out? Okay, not part of His plan. So then why didn't He give them asbestos suits to wear? Okay, asbestos wasn't invented yet. Why, why, why? Well, I have what I think is an interesting theory. I believe that God wanted the onlookers to see His power united with their faith so that all would know that when the two are mixed something miraculous can and will happen. God would not have let them go into the fire if they hadn't faith enough to withstand the trial. To the king they said, "We know the God whom we serve is able to deliver us from the fiery furnace, but if not . . . we still won't bow down." And to His faithful followers God says, "If you can't stand the heat, I won't let you be tossed into a furnace which I know will consume you. I'll be there with you." It was a multi-faceted lesson for all involved. He showed them that He had the power to save them, even if He didn't spare them from having to face the heat. He also went in with them. And maybe that's the lesson He's attempting to teach you in your hot trial. The lesson that deliverance doesn't mean avoidance. He may not allow you to avoid the heat, but He will enable you to withstand it . . . and moreover, He will be in the heat with you so that you come out with not so much as the smell of smoke on your clothing or singed hair. So you're in the furnace? Remember you can withstand it and you will come out *changed* but unharmed. Those three young men came out of that furnace stronger, more faithful, hopeful, and determined to continue to serve the God who delivered them. That old saying, "If you can't stand the heat," ends with the admonition to "stay out of the kitchen." Well, if you ask me, I believe the instruction should be, "If you can't stand the heat, STAY IN the kitchen" until God reveals His power to change, strengthen, and infuse you with faith. You know I always have to give my practical, personal application, right? So, here goes. My mother used to press my sisters' and my hair. It was a painful process as she pulled the incredibly hot pressing comb through our hair—especially if we dared move. Many times I wore the marks of my 'branding' on my ears when I failed to heed my mother's warning to "be still." The hair on the back of our heads, near the neck, was referred to as "the kitchen," and was most difficult to press. It was hard to remain still while having that area pressed. My mother would tell us to hold still so that she could straighten the kitchen. We knew that we had to stand the heat while she was in the "kitchen." We struggled to obey, fearing being burned, but we had to trust her. When she was finished, the shiny, lovely, smooth hair made the trial in the heat worthwhile. What does getting your hair pressed have to do with going through a fiery trial? Those who have had their hair pressed already know the answer, but for the rest . . . enduring heat for the purpose of desired change is always worthwhile. Spiritually, if we, like the three boys, can stand strong, trust God, and face the fire for the sake of obedience to God, the end result will be beautiful.

Of Eagles and Pigeons

But they that wait upon the LORD shall renew their strength; they shall mount up with wings as eagles. Isaiah 40:31

If you dare to open your eyes to things around you, it's amazing the illustrations God gives us in life. Sometimes we may be struggling to find the answer to a complex issue and the answer is right in front of us. Only we're not looking for it in the obvious. We sometimes think that a complex problem must have a complex answer. Not so. Having dropped my daughter off with a friend who watched her for me after school, I was en route back to work. I was dealing with a really complicated matter in my life and desperate for an answer as to how to handle it. As I drove along, my gaze went to the sky above the highway where a large bird was flying. As I looked more closely, I realized it was a Bald Eagle. Its beauty made me hold my breath. There it was, soaring on the wind, majestically. It was almost like a dance. Its broad wingspan stretching against the grey sky. Its white head and tail like adornments on a dignitary. This stately creature barely flapped its wings, but instead used the wind to allow him to glide. It was truly a thing of beauty to behold. Then I saw another flock of birds just a few feet away in the sky. They were flying lower than the eagle, and definitely more clumsily. They were pigeons. I couldn't help noticing how they were fighting against the wind, and losing. The wind seemed to batter and beat up on them. They struggled to stay in the sky as the whipping wind knocked them about. They flapped their short wings feverishly and it seemed the more they flapped, the less stable they were. They were exhausting themselves trying to fight against the fury of the wind; meanwhile the eagle *used* the wind. The contrast was stark. Just then, my answer came to me. In my problematic situation I had been like the pigeons. I was fighting against the winds of change and exhausting myself. I was flapping my wings and making my circumstances less stable. I needed to be like the eagle and learn to allow the wind to propel me onward and upward. Maybe I needed to rise a little higher. We all have a choice to make when enduring the winds of strife. We can either be eagles or pigeons. If we wait upon the Lord, our strength will be renewed and we will be able to fly like eagles. That same passage in Isaiah gives us the assurance that we will also be able to run and not get weary and walk and not keel over. Every life is bound to have windy days . . . windy times. But if we will take a lesson from the eagle, we will not be beaten by the wind, but instead carried by it, gracefully. I don't know what problem you are facing in your life, but I do know that God has an answer for you. It may just be right in front of your face. Dare to look . . . and then dare to soar.

Let Down Your Net

Now when he had left speaking, he said unto Simon, Launch out into the deep, and let down your nets for a draught. And Simon answering said unto him, Master, we have toiled all the night, and have taken nothing: nevertheless at thy word I will let down the net. And when they had this done, they enclosed a great multitude of fishes: and their net break. Luke 5:4-6

When everything that you are trying to do is coming up empty, perhaps it's time to listen to Jesus and let down your net. The scene described in today's passage of scripture focuses on failure that prompted some fishermen to give up. Jesus had been preaching and he reached a certain lake where he saw two fishing boats, but the fishermen had given up and called it quits because they couldn't catch anything . . . not even a cold. Fishing was their livelihood, their primary source of income and yet they had failed to make a decent catch after working all night and into the day so they threw up their hands, pulled up their nets and went back to shore. Jesus then called out to Simon and told him to go back and let down their nets in deeper water. Simon was like any one of us who has been frustrated by failure followed by advice. He tells Jesus that he's been fishing all night and pulled up nothing more than a tire, a deflated basketball, and a pair of rusted bicycle handle bars. Nevertheless, he says he'll listen to Jesus and give it one more try. Here's a tip for you; listening to Jesus is always a good idea. When Simon drops his nets this time, in deeper water, he pulls them back up so full of fish that they break. The catch was so large that they had to beckon friends to help them. They filled up two boats and the weight of the fish was so heavy it nearly sank them. Talk about a fish story! In that moment failure met with Godly power and the result was astonishing. The fishermen had given up before Jesus gave them the simple instructions on how to succeed. Go deeper. And now the focus shifts to you. You feel like giving up. Perhaps you have failed at something important to you . . . maybe even your livelihood, small business, ministry, marriage, schooling. You've toiled all night on more than one occasion and you feel you have nothing to show for it. Why bother to continue trying with your apparent exercise in futility? You feel like these fishermen felt. But God is giving you the same instructions He gave to them. Go deeper and try again. We, like those fishermen, have thrown our nets into knee deep water and pulled them up empty. We've put our effort into it, but not our heart. We're trying to catch a job, a spouse, a home, a career, a blessing . . . but we can't seem to catch a break. So God comes along and gives us some advice. He says, you need to go deeper. How deep is your desire? How deep is your willingness to do God's will, God's way? Is ours a shallow desire to merely succeed or make money? Maybe it's a lust for popularity. We want our friends and family to be impressed when they see how well we're doing. So God says, cast your net deeper. Jesus is calling us out of the shallow water into the deep. Once we, by faith, go deeper, he'll tell us to let down our nets again and when we bring them back up they'll be bursting with blessings. Our hunger should be to do God's will for us. If our labors are coming up unfulfilled, maybe we're not deep enough. Follow the Master's advice and venture out into deeper water where your dependence will solely be on Him and His power. He will take you deeper and fill your nets to bursting.

Turbulence

Preserve me, O God: for in thee do I put my trust. Psalm 16:1

I was on board a flight from Seattle to Minneapolis, en route to a conference in Atlanta. There was nothing extraordinary about this flight; or so I thought. I settled in for the ride, pulled out my music and planned to sleep. Seated behind me were a mother and her two small children. As I dozed, I heard this woman reading a story to her children and conversing with them about good and bad influences spoken of in this book, their munchkin voices offering childish responses. It was adorable. I thought, "How sweet. She's teaching them values at such an early age." It was a heartwarming scene to which I drifted off to sleep. Some time later, the rough movement of the plane awakened me. In a state of partial awareness, I again heard this mother and her children. She spoke in calm, reassuring tones. The children were not afraid because their mother was there with them and her words gave them the assurance that everything would be all right. As the pilot attempted to land the plane, strong winds thrust the aircraft about, as if it were a roller coaster. Many passengers, myself included, sounded as if we were at Six Flags over Minneapolis. "Whoa!" we said in unison. There were other exclamations, which I won't mention. But these children, seated behind me laughed and giggled along with their mother. I must admit that I chuckled too in response to the dips and motion and the behavior of the other passengers. Being a kid at heart, I felt like throwing both my hands up to really enjoy the ride. These children, this mother and I were not afraid. We made the best of the turbulence and found a way to get through it . . . even with a little laughter and joy. Each life will include some turbulence. It will feel like things are out of control, as God, the Pilot, works to rectify your life—the aircraft. The ride may seem rough and bumpy. But the reassuring words spoken to us by our Heavenly Father should bring peace to our hearts and even a smile to our faces amid the dips, bumps, and motion.

As we disembarked, I playfully thanked the pilots and flight crew for the roller coaster ride. They laughed. I was partly serious, though. I had experienced a spiritual lesson through this turbulent ride. No matter how bumpy it gets, God is there to speak words of comfort. He is also in control of the ride. Throw your hands up!

What He Really Wants

Wherefore the Lord said, Forasmuch as this people draw near me with their mouth, and with their lips do honor me, but have removed their heart far from me, and their fear toward me is taught by the precept of men: Isaiah 29:13

Have you ever heard the expression he or she "talks a good game"? This saying describes a person who says all the right things but fails in the area of authenticity. They may say just what you want to hear, they may agree with you and talk about all that they plan to do in the way of support, yet they don't really mean it and in the end that sad fact becomes evident. The reason is that their heart really wasn't in it. It's mere "lip service," if you will. What I would much prefer is action motivated by a sincere heart. Not pleasing words that mean nothing. God is commiserating with us about this very problem in Isaiah 29. The people are praising Him with their lips . . . singing beautiful songs of His merit, jumping and shouting in church, talking about His goodness and even attending every church meeting. But their hearts are not in it. They are giving Him their time, their talent, perhaps even their money, but they have not yet given Him that one thing that He truly desires . . . their heart. Maybe they're obeying His commandments routinely, not out of love, rather out of religious obligation. I've seen it on more than one occasion. May even have been guilty of it myself. Our relationship with God becomes like a stale marriage. We get so caught up in the rituals that sometimes we neglect the nuptials. Sure you come home every night. You mindlessly kiss your spouse on the cheek and ask how their day went, responding "That's good, honey," even before they actually tell you what kind of day they had. You say thank you for dinner and give them a peck on the lips before slipping off into slumber. The next day, it's the same thing. You're in it, but your heart really isn't. You may even give your spouse gifts and words of praise, but your heart isn't as close as you know it should or could be. Rekindling and an awakening are needed. Stopping to pay attention to the attributes and reasons why your spouse is so wonderful and precious is a good place to start. When we pause to take in the wonder of who God is and we then compare that to who we are and contemplate how, exactly, it is that He could love us, our hearts will be drawn to Him. We give Him our works, but not our hearts. I know numerous individuals who have dedicated their life's work to God, but have a hard time dedicating their hearts to Him. They talk a good game . . . even do a great job for Him, but their respect for Him is taught, not wrought. I know that there have been times when I have led Praise and Worship because there was no one else to do it. But my heart wasn't in it because my mind was elsewhere or I was tired or just didn't feel like doing it. I later felt foolish when I considered the fact that Jesus most likely didn't feel like walking the road to Calvary for me. He was tired, and there was no one else to do it, but He did it out of love . . . His heart was in it. This has changed my attitude. We can give God so much and find in the end that we really have given Him nothing because we have failed to give Him our hearts. Some of the biggest devils are most talented in the exercise of Praise and Worship. And people who have no real relationship with God are just theatrical enough to preach some powerful sermons. The talent doesn't always reflect the condition of the heart. As one Bible writer puts it, "Having a form of godliness, but denying the power thereof: from such turn away." (2 Timothy 3:5) They sing beautifully, it would seem, for the Lord and say all the right things. But all it amounts to is a performance if the heart is not in it. I don't want to win an Academy Award for best actress for my performance as a Christian. I'll give God my whole heart and rejoice in the fact that He actually wants it. Just imagine; a perfect and powerful God wants our hearts. Go figure. He desires to be with you and loves you so much that He's willing to take you as you are and love you into shape. He doesn't just want your words of flattery, he wants you. He wants your heart. Revelation 3:20—Behold, I stand at the door, and knock: if any man hear my voice, and open the door, I will come in to him, and will sup with him, and he with me.

Tears Fall Up

My friends scorn me: but mine eye poureth out tears unto God.
Job 16:20

Our sorrows connect us with God. Did you know that? The proof is in Psalm 34 where the Word tells us that a broken spirit and a contrite heart are two of the human conditions to which God draws nigh. Unlike with some people who have an aversion to our tears and sorrow, when we are hurting and broken, God is drawn to us. He doesn't pull away or move far from us because we are in a bad spot or going through a rough patch. I once had a terrible experience in church and rushed to the ladies room where I stood sobbing. One by one, women of the church who entered the restroom and saw me, turned and scurried out. Not one paused to see if there was anything they could do to console me. Our tears are not an aversion to God. He feels the pain and sees the tears that fall from our eyes and is drawn to us by them. So, in a sense, our tears fall up. Defying the laws of gravity, the liquid sorrow falls upward to heaven, where the Lord is intently watching you, His child, and eager to dry your weeping eyes. His concern is so great that he recognizes the sound of your cry, like a mother knows that of her own baby, and He moves into action. It's as if the teardrops fall on Him like raindrops, yet He doesn't run for cover, instead He runs to our rescue. No doubt I am in the company of many who have, like David, cried enough to end a drought. Psalm 6:6 *says, "I am weary with my groaning; all the night make I my bed to swim; I water my couch with my tears."* I feel you, David. I'm reminded of many nights when I have cried what I thought were lonely tears, only to slowly become conscious of the fact that I was somehow being comforted. Eventually, my tears dissipated and as I reflect on it now, I cannot tell you when it happened, but my pain eased as well. I suspect it had little to do with anything external or natural. It wasn't any pill I took or deep breathing exercises I employed. In fact, any attempt of my own design would have served only to make me feel worse since my own actions were likely at the root of my initial pain. But the tears I cried, and the tears you cry, like our sorrows, connect us with God. Even if you feel like you've been crying for what seems like forever and the end of your tears doesn't seem to be in sight, God feels the moisture. He sees and will bring you comfort. We may not know exactly when or how, but we can be exact in knowing that He will. Were this not the case, I would be crying right now as I write these words of encouragement to you. Just as He has dried my tears, He will do the same for you. Your hurt is His hurt. Your pain; His pain. Your tears fall up and connect you with heaven, my friend. So cry if you must, but trust God to bring an end to the sorrow and He'll even go a step further. He will allow those tears to serve as water for the joy that will eventually spring up. *They that sow in tears shall reap in joy." Psalm 126:5*

Homemade gods

When the people saw that Moses delayed to come down from the mountain, the people gathered themselves together to Aaron, and said to him, "Up, make us gods, who shall go before us; as for this Moses, the man who brought us up out of the land of Egypt, we do not know what has become of him." Exodus 32:1

There the Children of Israel stood at the base of the mountain. Moses had ascended to get a word from God for them. They were standing in the very shadow of the God of the Universe. This God had delivered them from slavery and Pharaoh. This same God had opened the Red Sea, giving them the red carpet treatment from bondage to freedom. This God had provided for them a pillar of fire by night and a column of smoke by day as a guide through the wilderness. This God had revealed Himself time and time again. Yet, they grew frustrated and impatient, and someone came up with a bright idea to solve their waiting problem. "Hey, I know, let's just make our own God." "Yeah!" the crowd foolishly agreed, and with cheers and applause, the idiotic plan was underway. They stripped off all their jewelry and brought it to Aaron to be melted down and fashioned in the form of a god, which they could control. A Johnny on the Spot god. A lickety-split god. Their very own golden god. Aaron cooperated (we won't even discuss how Aaron could have taken such a leave of his senses) and Voila! They had an instant god. How ridiculous, huh? Well, before you agree and join me in ridiculing these irrational and impatient problem children, let's think about this for a second. How many times have we taken matters into our own hands and tried to shape or reshape our circumstances? Okay, so we haven't melted down the silverware or candleholders to make our own calf to worship and to tell how to bless us. But we've become impatient and tried to figure out how to work out our problems. And maybe we've even told God how to bless us. In essence we are saying, "You're taking too long, God, I'll just go ahead and work this out for myself." In so doing, we erect our golden calf. And our golden calf has about as much power as the one erected that day in the middle of the desert. If that's not enough, we then even make gods of things to serve as substitutes for waiting. Rather than patiently wait for the blessing that God has designed for us, we go ahead and devise a substitute that will tie us over until He comes through. That substitute sometimes gets in the way of what God had for us and may have been poised to deliver had we not opted for the do-it-yourself model. So let's put our scoffing and pompous query, "How could they possibly have been so silly" back on the shelf and let's take another look at this scene. These recently liberated slaves, new on the freedom scene, had been accustomed to a life of following orders. Although under the rule of cruel Egyptian taskmasters, who ruled with whips and torture, their lives were at least organized and regimented. It may have been a grievous way to live, but they knew what to expect. Now they were in this desert at the mercy of God and this man, Moses, who had led them to freedom, but who also led them away from what they knew. And now, he too was MIA. They had waited more than 200 years to be delivered from Egypt, but now they couldn't wait a few days to receive direction from the God who set them free. Clearly in their desperation they forgot who God was and what He could do. Waiting can bring out the worst in us without the element of patience. When something upsets the pattern of our lives and we are forced to wait for God to come through, there will sometimes be the temptation to handle it ourselves. If we give in to that temptation the devil will be all too happy to give us instructions on how to make a golden calf. And we can be sure that our method of working things out with our homemade god will fail. So why not just wait for the real God to remedy your problem? Following that afternoon episode of, "Aaron, the Foolish Crowd and the Golden Cow," those same players made several more "you've got to be kidding" choices. Choices that caused them to wander in the desert for 40 years. Finally, they got enough of a grip on the true God, that He led them to the land He had promised. By then, Moses was so disgusted with them that he messed up and missed out on the grand entrance himself. That's another story for another time.

Happy Birthday!

Even to your old age I am He, and to gray hairs I will carry you. I have made, and I will bear; I will carry and will save.
Isaiah 46:4

I hate birthdays. Well, let me clarify that. I love celebrating other people's birthdays, but I really don't like my own. I don't know exactly why. Maybe it's because for me birthdays don't really signify the beginning of something, but rather the end. The end of youth, opportunity, childbearing years, a healthy and energetic metabolism, a fighting chance in the battle of the fat cells. I don't know, it just seems like most of the good things begin to decline the older we get. Let's not even mention the body's tendency to succumb to the laws of gravity. Some love to quote the phrase, "You're not getting older, you're getting better." They, obviously, are drunk on Geritol or suffering from early dementia. Maybe they're just trying to convince themselves that they don't mind growing older. Well, I do. And for that reason, I hate my birthday. Now, don't get me wrong, the alternative to getting old is far less favorable, as far as I'm concerned, but I still don't like the idea of aging. I just don't. When I turned 30, it was down hill from there. And each year I faced my birthday with more dread than the last. When I finally hit 40, I thought I would surely die from depression. Not only did I dye my hair jet black, but considered drinking my Miss Clairol. At 47, it's apparent I didn't die, but not for lack of trying. Seems turning 40 isn't as deadly as I thought. But, the thought of turning 50 brings with it shutters of despair that make a panic attack seem like a midday nap. Yet in the midst of my grief and woe concerning birthdays, I have the nerve to appreciate life. What a contradiction, wouldn't you say? To hate getting older, but love living. As a Christian the contradiction seems all the greater. But I remind myself that the Christian is not perfect . . . he or she is human. And as human beings, there will always be weak areas of our spiritual consciousness through which God gets our attention and shows us where we need to trust Him more. My grim view of birthdays is one of those areas. Every one of us has one. For David it wasn't birthdays, but enemies. For Paul, it wasn't birthdays but pride. For Peter it wasn't birthdays but doubt. The key is in recognizing and relinquishing. In order to move forward in our blessings we must identify our weaknesses and then be strong enough to give them to God. My disdain for birthdays does not diminish my appreciation for the fact that God has preserved me and sustained me for all the years of my life. I simply have issues that only He can rectify. There, I said it. And the marvelous news is that He CAN rectify my every sorrow and relieve me of my burdens. He can do the same for you. Do you have your own version of birthday anxiety? Why not give it to God and let Him change your outlook? This is what I'm committing to on this day, August 27th, which just so happens to be my . . . you guessed it, birthday. I can't in good conscience sing the words to the hymn, *I Surrender All*, one more time without at least making an attempt to actually do so. The Word of God puts it this way, *"Cast all your cares upon Him for He cares for you."* (1 Peter 5:7) Yes, He even cares about the gray hairs we color in attempts to maintain the appearance of youth . . . . He has numbered them, in fact. So give Him your concerns today and learn to walk in the newness of life. And then together we can sing, Happy New-Birth-day to you.

Lost

Then shall ye call upon me; and ye shall go and pray unto me, and I will hearken unto you. And ye shall seek me and find me when ye shall search for me with all your heart. Jeremiah 29:12-13

The department store was called G. Fox & Company, and it was, for me, a magical wonderland, especially at Christmas. Each year, my parents would take us on the hour-long drive to the big city of Hartford to see the Christmas lights at Constitution Plaza and all along Main Street. We would then make our way to G. Fox & Company, where each of the older children would be given an allowance for Christmas shopping. While my siblings were old enough to shop alone and would take with them my sister, Marionette, who was 2 years older than me, I had to stay with my mother. She kept me mildly in check with promises that we would eventually get to the toy department. My siblings were given their marching orders and told to meet us at a certain time, in a certain location. As they all darted off in different directions, I stood by my mother, looking longingly at the ones who had been set free. "Don't worry, we'll get to the toy department," my mother continuously promised, sensing the increase in my level of disappointment, "I just want to look at a few things first." Knowing my propensity to wander, she told me to stay close enough to her that I could see her at all times. She repeated these instructions again, to make sure I understood. As we mulled through the linen, housewares, and women's departments, she periodically reassured me that we weren't far from the toy department. Finally, we made our way to the children's department and, at last, I caught a glimpse of my promised land . . . the toy department! One peek at the huge stuffed animals and dolls and I lost all sense and sensibility. My mother had also become engrossed in her own "deal finding" expedition. I took one step in the direction of the toy land and could now more clearly see my long awaited destination. One more step and then another. I looked back, remembering what my mother had said, "Make sure you can see me at all times." I could still see her, so I took another step toward Oz and before I knew it, I wasn't in Kansas anymore. There I was in the middle of toy heaven. There were bikes and baby dolls, large toy soldiers and racing cars . . . Oh, what joy! Then I remembered my mother. I looked back and there was no sight of her. My pleasure erupted into panic. The once beautiful stuffed animals became lions and tigers and bears . . . oh, my. Fear gripped me and I ran to an adult to ask if they could help me find my mother. I was taken to the department store office, given a lollipop and told they would find my mother. They paged her and soon a likewise panicked mom walked through the door and whisked me into her arms and hugged me. When she loosened her grip enough for me to catch a breath, I announced, "Mommy, you were lost, I'm glad they found you!" Of course I had it in reverse, but the comic relief was enough to calm her nerves and save me from sure punishment. I hadn't intended to lose sight of my mother that evening and I didn't make an all out dash toward the toy department. Inch by inch, I made my way there, and wound up lost. I was so focused on the thing I wanted, I lost sight of the one I needed. I often reflect on that childhood experience and think about how so many may wind up lost without intending to do so. We're inching away from God, one step at a time, moving in the direction of the things we desire and away from Him. It's not our intention to lose sight of Him, but step-by-step we risk winding up lost. Before we know it, we look for Him and He's out of view. Yet, like my mother, He is looking for us and if we'll be still and call for Him, He will come and whisk us up into His arms. If you're drifting, here's a novel idea . . . stop where you are, ask for Help and wait for the Father to find you.

Our Light Affliction …

*For our light affliction, which is but for a moment, worketh for us
a far more exceeding and eternal weight of glory; While we look not
at the things which are seen, but at the things which are not seen:
for the things which are seen are temporal; but the things which are
not seen are eternal.*

2 Corinthians 4:17-18

When I'm having an exceptionally difficult time I often tell myself,
"This is temporary, Linda." The self-reminder gives me just enough
reassurance to hang in there. My mother used to say, "this too shall
pass." And it's true. Everything comes to an end at some point. The
hard part is in getting to that point. Yes, that's where it gets a bit tricky.
If we could fast forward to the end of a bad time, like with a DVD, or
skip scenes we don't like, that would be wonderful, wouldn't it? But,
unfortunately, life is not a movie. We do, however, have a preview of
the ending that can make us hold on. That ending also makes whatever
we're going through seem small and short-lived. Against the backdrop
of eternity, our present suffering is minuscule. The key is to focus on
things eternal. Don't look at what you see, but look at eternity. I hear
you saying, "So I'm not supposed to look at what I see, but what I don't
see? How is that even possible?" The answer is, by faith. Since faith
is the substance of things hoped for and the evidence of things not
seen, by faith we can see what is not readily visible. Like the survival
from terminal illness or the restoration of a broken home. While these
afflictions are excruciating, the Word says when compared to the glory
that we will one day experience, they are light. Faith requires that we
see them as light and temporary. No, God doesn't mean to make light
of what we are going through, He just wants us to see our problems in

contrast to the glorious end. In this case, the end will definitely justify the means. Pregnancy is an example of this kind of hope. The bloating, swollen feet, morning sickness, and other discomforts . . . including the chief hardship, labor, are painful. In the midst of the experience, we wish for a swift end to it all. Many vow to never endure such again, and mean it. But when the precious child is laid in the arms of the proud parents, all of the pain and suffering is erased. The agonies were temporary and cannot be compared to the joy. Like the moment the degree is placed in the hand of the graduate or the runner crosses the finish line, the glorious end makes light the affliction. The end of a thing is better than the beginning, according to the Word. So, with renewed hope, we look to that end and draw upon the strength that comes from knowing the end will come.

Empty Apologies

For godly sorrow worketh repentance to salvation not to be repented of: but the sorrow of the world worketh death. II Corinthians 7:10

Some people find it hard to apologize. For others, the words, "I'm sorry" seem to roll off their tongues with ease, yet the words prove to be what you might call an empty apology. This is an apology that has no meaning because the person offering it truly isn't sorry. How do you know their apology is insincere? Because it brings with it no change. If a person winds up having to apologize for the same thing over and over again, eventually you realize that they really aren't sorry . . . at least not sorry enough to stop doing whatever it is that creates the need for an apology. These types of apologies are what Paul is referring to in the admonition made to the people of Corinth in the above text. He is saying the kind of sorrow expressed in the world has no life giving or restorative qualities. It merely leads to death. But the type of sorrow, which God sparks in our hearts for the things we've done, now THAT works to salvation. Not the sorrow experienced just because we got caught. But the genuine sorrow that makes us want to live differently, better, right . . . that is Godly sorrow. Repentance is a result of it. The world has taught us to say whatever is convenient and productive. Even if it isn't necessarily true, the way of the world is to say whatever is necessary to generate the desired results. Sometimes saying we are sorry, when we really aren't, is convenient . . . or just a con. But God cannot be fooled. He wants to see change coming out of our apologies for the things we've done wrong. Without reformation and a turning away from the things for which we claim to be sorry, our words are nothing more than vocal chord exercise. If we find ourselves repenting for the same things over and over, guess what? We haven't really repented. Confessing and apologizing are the first steps in the process of conversion. At some point we have to actually change. I have received apologies from people who made no effort to show me that they were indeed sorry for the pain or hurt they caused me. It left me feeling all the more hurt. When we go to God with words of regret, we need to be prepared to back those words up with action. And only God can give us the strength to make good on our apologies. Perhaps you've struggled with the ability to change, despite your feelings of regret. There are things in your life over which you truly desire to gain victory. Say this prayer with me:

> Father, I'm truly sorry for the failed attempts to overcome. I've told you that I'm sorry more than once, and slipped back into my old ways. But today, right now, I am asking for your Spirit to help me change and make me what I should be. I repent and surrender to you and your will.
> In Jesus' Name, Amen.

Up until now maybe you've been offering empty apologies because you thought you could change on your own. Or maybe you thought saying "I'm sorry" was enough. In answer to the prayer you just offered, may God accept your heartfelt apology and give you grace to continue in victory and peace.

It's an Emergency!

And call upon me in the day of trouble: I will deliver thee, and thou shalt glorify me.

Psalm 50:15

Calling 911 is an action reserved for emergency situations. It alerts authorities of critical situations and sends, with dispatch, help from various agencies, such as the police and fire departments. Within minutes rescue workers are on the scene, rendering emergency services. One call and suddenly there are paramedics or fire fighters, ambulances, police cars or fire trucks converging on the scene with flashing lights and sirens. Frenzied efforts are made to help the person in crisis . . . all because someone called 911. In Psalms, the 40th chapter, starting at verse 13, David is calling 911. "Be pleased, O God to deliver me: O Lord, make haste to help me." It's an emergency for him. He continues, "Let them be ashamed and confounded together that seek after my soul to destroy it; let them be driven backward and put to shame that wish me evil." His emergency is not so much a physical threat, although he has his share of those from his enemies, but at this moment he is concerned about those who want to drive him to ruin and ultimately destroy him. David's urgent appeal to God is that he stop the wicked from being able to rejoice over him and laugh at his grief. "Let them be desolate for a reward of their shame that say unto me, Aha, aha." In other words, let those who laugh at me in the midst of my problems receive ruin as their reward. This 911 call ends with David asking God not to tarry in helping him. God takes David's emergency call seriously and He responds. And God takes seriously every emergency call made by His children. We may not always see an immediate response to our call for help, but I believe there is a frenzy of activity in heaven. Here is what the Lord promises, *"He shall call upon me, and I will answer him: I will be with him in trouble . . ." Psalm 91:15* God is fully aware of our need for emergency help. I have called on Him many times in my desperation and I am certain that it was His help that pulled me through. In crisis, we need to be assured that help is on the way. Imagine calling 911 and waiting for a response but receiving none. News reports once focused on a small boy who called 911 to get help for his mother who was not breathing. In the tape recording of his call, he pleaded for someone to come and help his mother. The dispatcher on the other end of the phone discounted his plea for help and coldly told him to stop playing. She hung up on him. The boy persisted, calling back. When rescue workers were finally sent to the scene, they found the boy's account to be true and his mother, sadly, had not survived. His mother had instructed the boy that if anything ever happened, he should call 911. He had done just as she said, but his call was not taken seriously. Such is not the case with the Father. He has instructed us of what to do if anything should ever happen. He says, "Call upon Me." Because He is in tune with our lives, He is fully aware of how serious our situation may be. The help that He renders is the help that we need. Perhaps not always the type of help we want, but certainly what is best for us. And His response time is in accordance with His will and His knowledge of the situation. In an emergency you can ask God to make haste to help you. Then wait and trust. Heaven is busy working to deliver you. Your call is not being ignored.

Arrivals and Departures

For the Lord himself shall descend from heaven with a shout . . . then we shall be caught up to meet the Lord in the air: and so shall we ever be with the Lord. I Thessalonians 4:16-17 (paraphrased)

Airports are a scene of great emotion. I sat in my car on the lower level of the Seattle airport awaiting the arrival of my dear friend and the scene that played out before me brought tears to my eyes. Dozens of people stood on the sidewalk, looking anxiously for the familiar face of the person coming to get them. The moment at which they saw the car or the person they recognized, expressions of joy, excitement, and sometimes relief settled on their faces. Husbands were reunited with wives, children with parents, siblings, friends and relatives greeting each other. There were hugs and kisses, smiles and laughter. I watched a woman get out of her car and walk to a tall young man with her arms outstretched to embrace him. An older couple smiled when they looked at each other, a long hug followed. One after another, gestures of love and affection played out like the happy ending of a story. I thought about the scene playing out one level up at the departure area. There were hugs and kisses there also, but the scene was sadder, no doubt. Goodbyes aren't usually as happy as hellos. What a contrast between these arrivals and departures. Finally, my friend emerged from the airport, luggage in tow. I was equally as happy to see her as the others who greeted their loved ones. We shared our own hugs and headed home. Now, I've spent a lot of time in airports, but this was the first time I'd actually paid attention to this beautiful display of love. It made me think of another such event that is on the distant horizon. Another time of arrivals and departures. Imagine the scene, if you will. There we will stand, waiting for our loved One. The One who is actually coming to receive us. And what a grand arrival it will be. And some of us will even take flight. Think of it as a celestial airport. The One we are waiting for will come in the clouds of glory . . . in the air, and then we will take our transport. I could almost shout about it right now. There will be joyous hellos and embraces on one level. But there will be sad departures on another level because some will be left behind. Just like at the airport, that departure will not be such a happy sight. Knowing this, God has a remedy. He has promised to wipe ever tear from our eyes. Still, my heart's desire is that every one of my loved ones, and you, the one who is reading this, will celebrate the arrival and not mourn the departure. Let's all be caught up.

Living Out Our Commitments

Commit thy way unto the Lord; trust also in him; and he shall bring it to pass. Psalm 37:5

When my daughter was 13 years old she was baptized at the close of a revival at our church. Having made the decision she wanted to follow Christ, I supported her wholeheartedly. When my pastor and friend plunged her beneath the water, lifted her and kissed her on her face, my heart was filled to overflowing. I couldn't hold back the joyous tears. Later in the week, I shared the news with another friend and asked that she pray for my daughter as she tries to live out her commitment. That's when it really occurred to me that the act of faith on Saturday was really a life-long commitment. Sure, I was well aware of the seriousness of her decision when she first presented me with the idea during an appeal in church. During her Bible study, she was educated on the weight of this outward show of her love for God. The step was not taken lightly. Yet, living it out would require a continual, step-by-step commitment. So far, she's happily living out her commitment to Jesus, but what about 10 years from now? Will she still have the same eagerness and zeal about her decision as she did on the day she stood and took her baptismal vows? I pray so. I know that there have been times when I haven't exactly demonstrated the best example of one living out my commitment to the Lord. I've had good days and bad days, good years and bad years. In life we make commitments and at the onset we are earnest in our performance of the promise or vow. Then as time moves on, we sometimes become less zealous. There are even times we completely abandon the commitment . . . a few diets come to mind. However, if we can live out our commitments one day at a time, we have the hope of success. And if the overall trend of our lives reflects a determination to be committed, we, again, have hope of success. Should we approach each day with a renewed effort to live according to what we have promised God, then we can honestly say that we are living out our commitment. During the revival I spoke of earlier, the speaker said something that gave me a great deal of encouragement in my commitment walk. He said that righteousness isn't always doing what's right, all the time. Righteousness is doing what's right "this" time. Committed living, likewise, takes place one instance, one day, one step at a time. Each day tell yourself that you will live for Him today.

Beauty for Ashes

To appoint unto them that mourn in Zion, to give unto them beauty for ashes, the oil of joy for mourning, the garment of praise for the spirit of heaviness; that they might be called trees of righteousness, the planting of the Lord, that he might be glorified. Isaiah 61:3

Poet Laureate Maya Angelou tells of how she was sexually molested at age 8 by her mother's boyfriend. As any child should, she told of this violation. Her nine-year-old brother was her confidante. When word of her attack made its way to adults, a group of angry individuals hunted the man down and kicked him to death. News of this man's end compounded the tragedy for her and she felt that her words had caused his death. For this reason, she did not speak for 5 years. Certainly she was not responsible for the despicable act played upon her by this person. Nor was she to blame for the actions of the vigilantes who brought him to what they felt was justice. Still, her self-inflicted guilt sentenced her to 5 years of silence. When she finally broke her silent exile and again spoke, a well of beauty sprang forth from her heart, through her mouth and her pen. She had let the silent pain erupt into a crescendo of affirmation and exhortation. Her words became her heart's music, bringing rhyme and reason to the once silent anguish of her soul. Sweet repose now quieted the clamor of her hurtful past and hushed the white noise of her guilt. She later wrote, "I believe that each of us comes from the Creator, trailing wisps of glory." Imagine this powerful declaration coming from one who was once muted by emotional devastation. Not all of us have experiences so horrific as this. But each of us has something that has pained us deeply and thrust us into silent agony. We may utter no sound, but our spirit screams. God hears this inward, blood-curdling cry and seeks to hush it with soothing consolation that will give way to outward praise. He encourages us to put on the garment of praise for the spirit of heaviness and wants to give us beauty for ashes. I would love for something lovely to be born out of my pain. God can make that happen for us. Many of the Psalms penned by David echoed from a soul that felt empty. *Hear my cry, O God. Attend unto my prayer. From the end of the earth will I cry unto thee, when my soul is overwhelmed lead me to the rock that is higher than I (Psalm 61:1-2).* Some of the most beautiful songs have been written by those with broken hearts. And breathtaking paintings have materialized on canvas at the hands of artists whose paintbrushes were dipped in sorrow. Each song and painting a testimony of God's ability to give us the oil of joy for mourning. Just as much of Maya Angelou's poetry and prose glorifies God, so too can the fruit of our hardship. And when the silence of our pain is broken, the beautiful Name of Jesus will spill from our lips as a lovely ballad. May He heal your hurt today and bring about something wonderful to silence the anguish and amplify the praise.

Let Jesus Speak

"Now when he came nigh to the gate of the city, behold, there was a dead man carried out, the only son of his mother, and she was a widow: and much people of the city was with her. And when the Lord saw her, he had compassion on her, and said unto her, Weep not. And he came and touched the bier (or flat frame): and they that bare him stood still. And he said, Young man, I say unto thee, Arise. And he that was dead sat up, and began to speak. And he delivered him to his mother." Luke 7:12-15:

Words are powerful. They are the means by which thoughts are communicated, messages are delivered, facts are transmitted, ideas are shared, and instructions are disseminated. (I threw in that last one because the words sounded important.) Words generate action. And the words spoken are often made more important by the one who speaks them. Especially when it's Jesus. There are numerous accounts of the profound utterances of Jesus contained in the Bible. But let's look a just a few choice examples in the scriptures to get you through today. First, look at John, chapter 5:5-9, by the famous pool of Bethesda. *"And a certain man was there, which had an infirmity thirty and eight years. Jesus saw him lie, and knew that he had been now a long time in that case, he saith unto him, Wilt thou be made whole? The impotent man answered him, Sir, I have no man, when the water is troubled, to put me into the pool: but while I am coming, another steppeth down before me. Jesus saith unto him, Rise, take up thy bed, and walk. And immediately the man was made whole, and took up his bed, and walked: and on the same day was the Sabbath."* (Applaud here!) Another takes place in *Matthew, 9: 2-7. "And, behold, they brought to him a man sick of the palsy, lying on a bed: and Jesus seeing their faith said unto the sick of the palsy; Son, be of good cheer; thy sins be forgiven thee . . . .*

Arise, take up thy bed, and go unto thine house. And he arose, and departed to his house." *(More applause!)* These are circumstances where HUGE problems are addressed by Jesus with few words. But those words have BIG results and bring about SUPER-CHARGED change. We all could use some positive change in our lives. So today my request is simple . . . Could you just . . . kinda, let Jesus speak? Yes, even to your HUGE problem. Because when Jesus speaks, healing occurs. Sometimes when we speak we injure. One word spoken by us can sometimes cause utter destruction. His words render amazing, miraculous results. When Jesus speaks, life is restored, lights come on, those who once had to be carried are suddenly able to leap and dance. When Jesus speaks, foolish babble is silenced. When Jesus speaks, we are forgiven. Let Jesus do the talking. Now for the pièce de résistance, look at today's key text from Luke 7. A young man is dead and his widowed mother is ready to jump into the grave with him, but Jesus has something to say about it . . . *"And he said, Young man, I say unto thee, Arise. And he that was dead sat up and began to speak"*. The text doesn't tell us what the young man said, although I'd like to think it was something wonderful, it just tells us that he "began to speak." He that was dead sat up and began to speak. Where there was death, there was now life. Jesus' words gave a second chance. He can speak life to your seemingly dead situation too. And so, as we draw attention to words, I think it would be beneficial if we would elect to choose words that render similar results . . . like "forgive me" and "I love you". In this way we let Jesus speak through us. Our words are His. First, He says to you . . . "Arise!"

Lessons From a Dog

. . . Lord, if thou wilt, thou canst make me clean. Luke 5:12

One warm, late summer day, my friend Susan decided to wash their family dog, Abby. Knowing it would be no simple task, my daughter Brooke and I offered to help. It had been a while since Sue and I had last bathed her, so we knew we had our work cut out for us. But after such a hot summer, surely, we thought, she'd love it. We had no idea just how challenging it would be. Rather than just using the hose, I suggested we fill the pail with warm soapy water to give her a soothing bath. With large bucket of water, dog shampoo and brushes in hand, we marched outside to launch Operation Abby Clean-up. We called her, and, as always, she came running. Being a loveable lab and who-knows-what mixture, she rolled over to enjoy our playful petting and praise, "Good girl!" She loved the attention and affirmations. But the moment we began to pour the water on, she became a different dog. Once playful, we now had to hold her down to begin the process of shampooing and brushing her. For a moment she seemed to enjoy the lathering as we massaged her coat. A little more water . . . she was nearly clean . . . and suddenly Abby went from Lassie to Cujo. She wrestled away from us, suds and all, and tore off in the direction of her dirt hole, which she had dug under a tree in the yard. There she began feverishly digging in the dirt, clouds of dust rising. "No, Abby! Why, Abby?" we screamed. But she kept right on digging. We called to her, and pleaded with her, "Here girl!" She ignored our calls and instead took off running in the opposite direction. For the next 30 minutes, we chased her, cajoled her, and whistled to her—patting on our legs for her to come to us. The scene must have resembled a Three Stooges movie, the three of us chasing a sudsy dog across the large back yard. "Here, girl!" we called. But off to the edge of the yard she ran, hiding underneath some brush. We pursued her and each time we nearly caught her, she would dart past us and lope in a different direction. Once or twice we had her, but she pulled away. At one point, I caught her by the collar and she dragged me across the yard. I was determined not to let go, but as I saw the ground rapidly approaching my face, I indeed let go. Sue, being her master, said, "Let me try. She always comes to me." Not this time. In a firm voice, she commanded, "Abby, you come here this instant!" Abby headed in her direction, as if to obey, then once inches outside her grasp, faked left and was off to the dirt hole again. Finally, she came close enough and we had her. We tried pulling her in the direction of our makeshift dog grooming shop, but she wouldn't budge. So, having had enough of this, I picked her up, and carried this heavy, smelly, wet, soapy (but even dirtier) dog across the yard. I put her down near the deck, straddled her and held her in place as we *again* washed her, rinsed her with warm water, washed her again, and brushed her. Finally, she laid still, allowing this baptism of sorts. At last, she was clean. We towel dried her and gave her a treat. This time she didn't head for the dirt hole again. She climbed into a chair on the deck, contentedly resting in the last rays of the afternoon sun, clean. We headed for the shower. As I recounted the experience later, of course you know I saw the spiritual angle. "Why, Abby?!" we cried. "Why, Linda?!" I thought. How many times have I returned to what I knew was not good for me? What would make me dirty. Even wallowed in it. (2 Peter 2:22—The dog is turned to his own vomit again; and the sow that was washed to her wallowing in the mire.) Many reading this, I'm sure, can relate. So often God attempts to clean up our lives and we run from Him, heading right back to our dirt hole. Yet, He pursues us with loving calls and outstretched hands. (Jeremiah 31:3—The Lord hath appeared of old unto me, saying, Yea, I have loved thee with an everlasting love: therefore with loving-kindness have I drawn thee.) If we get close enough to Him, He will pick us up and carry us to the place where we can be made clean. He doesn't want to harm us, but for some reason we fear the process. If we'd stop running and resisting, we would see that He only wants to groom us and wash away all the filth and dirt that the world has placed on us. Once we surrender, He will lather us with his love and rinse us with His peace. He'll even give us a treat . . . it's called salvation. Now clean, now content, we can rest in the warm rays of the "Son".

Rescue Me

The LORD was ready to save me: therefore we will sing my songs to the stringed instruments all the days of our life in the house of the LORD. Isaiah 38:20

Not all would admit it, but the idea of being rescued if need be is a welcome one. Those who are self-assured and self-sufficient, perhaps proud, and maybe even a little arrogant, might never want to own up to the fact that they may at some point need help desperately. Members of a particular gender, and I won't mention any names or specific groups, who hate to even ask for directions would certainly shrink at the thought of having to be rescued. Rambunctious teenagers who reach that age where they suddenly and miraculously know everything are also among those least likely to admit to needing help. The idea of being submissive brings with it a degree of shame for many. But each and every one of us will at some point need help and we should never allow pride or lofty attitudes to stand in the way of receiving the help we need. When, heeding the promptings of the Holy Spirit, I had decided to pick up and move from Connecticut to Washington State with my then 5-year-old daughter, the thought of such a major undertaking truly frightened me. What was equally frightening was the 4-day, cross-country journey that stretched eerily before me. The point at which the full magnitude of this decision finally set in, it launched me into a near panic. I would be leaving my father, family, and everything familiar behind on the East Coast and journeying to a land I knew not of. I felt like Abraham, except I had the luxury of a Toyota Camry to carry me, instead of camels and oxen, searing heat and flies. Still, I was afraid. Thoughts of rescue comforted me, however. With all the flaws that God has yet to work out in me, praise God admitting I need help isn't one of them. I made it very clear that if, at any point, I discovered that I was making a huge mistake and that perhaps what I thought was the Holy Spirit turned out to be a hallucination, I would yell, HELP! I told my father that if I got way out in the middle of who knows where Montana and had a melt-down, I was going to call him and say, "Come get me!" Yes, this grown woman was going to yell, "Daddy!" And what was most precious was the fact that my "Daddy" promised me that if I did call on him, he would drop everything and come and get me. I wasn't too proud to ask for help, and he wasn't too lofty to provide it. Reminds me of another Father/Child relationship. Jesus had made the decision to travel a great distance for an incredible undertaking. His Father stood by on-call, in the event that His Son wound up crying out for rescue. Thank God, literally, that He didn't. Otherwise we wouldn't even be here. But His Father was there. Even at the point where He felt forsaken, all heaven was ready to be dispatched if need be. The same rescue crew was on hand for me in the event I needed them. But, with the help of a friend, I made it to Seattle without caving in and calling on Daddy. Just knowing he was there was somehow enough. And so was my Heavenly Father. He's still standing by, poised to come to my rescue if and when I call upon Him. *Psalms 50:15—And call upon me in the day of trouble: I will deliver thee, and thou shalt glorify me.* And sometimes I do feel like crying out "Come get me!" to my Father above. When the cares of life press in on me and I feel stranded in the middle of nowhere in my existence, I want to cry out to Him, pleading that He come for me. I'm reassured by the knowledge that He one day will do just that. I pray that none of us will be too proud or arrogant to be rescued. The thought of being rescued gives me reason to sing!

Guess What?

Be not deceived, God is not mocked, whatsoever a man soweth, that shall he also reap.

Galatians 6:7

Today's scripture is both good and bad news . . . depending on which side you're on. The promise that we will reap what we sow is a glad tiding for some and a horrible threat for others. If we have sown seeds of kindness and love, then the return on that investment will be a wonderful blessing. The crop that springs up from decency is lush and bountiful. It nourishes and you can live on it. But the produce from the hate garden is bitter and poisonous. It's indeed bountiful, but it nourishes no one. I wonder why so many choose to eat of it. And when you sow, good or bad, the yield is generally larger than the planting. That's basically the nature of reaping. Not only do you harvest what you have planted, but in greater abundance. For example, you plant a seed and a tree springs up where that seed was placed in the ground. And on that tree are numerous pieces of fruit, which contain more seeds. If the initial seed was a healthy, good seed, the yield will be a welcome one. When it is time to be harvested, you will discover that what has grown out of what was sown is something to be proud of; like the prize winning apples at the county fair. Even that ridiculously weird looking, chemically enhanced 500 pound pumpkin that someone thought should be grown gains the attention of many and wins a prize. If you've grown good fruit, you'll wear your blue ribbon with pride. Bad seeds are equally productive and render similar harvests, but you won't be as happy at harvest time. And the fruit that springs up, just keeps on growing long after the initial seed is planted. The strongest weed killer isn't enough to stunt the growth of that harvest. Like a lie that grows out of control or hurtful words that produce far more grief than intended, you wish you could somehow stop the growth. The admonition of today's scripture is that we not be fooled. There's no getting around it. If you plant it, it will grow. Good or bad. Knowing this, you'd think we'd be more careful in our sowing.

Death Sentences

Let no corrupt communication proceed out of your mouth, but that which is good to the use of edifying, that it may minister grace unto the hearers. Ephesians 4:29

I considered her to be a dear friend. We had worked together in ministry and formed what I thought was a close bond of sisterhood. At different times in our friendship we had encouraged one another. Very much aware of the difficulties experienced by women in ministry we had vowed to always lift up one another, pray for each other, and do all that we could to aid the other in her spiritual pursuits. I had extended my help to her on many occasions, assisting her in her religious work. I trusted her and believed that she had my best interest at heart. When she came to me to report that another person who I considered to be a longtime friend of mine had been spreading falsehoods about me, I was saddened by the news but thankful that she had made me aware. With her information, she also advised me that she had instructed the person who spoke so ill of me to stop. Again, I thanked her. For months and even years, the rumors continued to circulate. Though grieved by the hate-fueled lies, I gave it to God and elected to let Him handle it. I attempted to speak to the spreader of the cruel untruths, but she fled, refusing to allow me to address the matter with her. Having made an effort to follow the Matthew 18 principle, I resigned to the idea that I had done my part and God would now have to do the rest. Another year passed. Thinking the rumor mill had shut down and gone out of business, I began to feel healing take place in my broken spirit. Then one night I was speaking with another dear friend when it was revealed that the true author of the lies was none other than the friend who had brought me the news in the first place. I was informed that the gossip had originated with her. I felt as if someone had socked me in the stomach with the strength of George Foreman. I sat in stunned silence. Thoughts of all that I had done for this woman flooded into my mind. The early mornings I was awakened by the ringing of my phone to find her on the other end asking for help or prayer or counsel. "I know I can always get a word from you, Lin. That's why I love you." I couldn't for the life of me understand what would prompt someone who claims to be your friend, to whom you have never done harm but only good, to spread untruths about you and scandalize your name. I was mortally wounded. All week I walked around in a fog. The news that this person who I thought supported and believed in me actually sought to destroy me, nearly did. This person whom I loved. Why would she? Why not? Satan desires to sift us as wheat. If for one moment we allow him to gain entrance, like an unwanted house guest or broke relative, he won't leave until he has succeeded at stirring up strife. If we don't keep our guard up, he can use us to try to bring down our fellow man . . . bringing *us* down in the process. When the apostle Paul made this admonition that the people of Ephesus shouldn't let corrupt communication or gossip come from their mouths it was because he knew the damage that idle chatter and lies would do not only to the victim but the person using their mouths as weapons. He knew the awful things said would be "death sentences." Words strung together that when fired from their mouths would be as deadly as rapidly fired ammo. These words could cause the death a person's character, reputation, peace and even ministry. And for this reason he ended the instruction with specific counsel. After advising them of what not to say, he told them exactly what to say. "Only that which edifies the hearer." There's your criterion in the decision on what to say. Will it curse someone or bless? Would you appreciate the same being said about you? Are these healing words or hurting words? Before you speak, take the test. If the rumors you are spreading were to make their way right back to you, would you be all right with the person you spoke of knowing you said it? Claiming Christianity requires putting your heart where your mouth is. James 1:26 says, *"If any man among you seem to be religious, and bridleth not his tongue, but deceiveth his own heart, this man's religion is vain."* Endnote: I have forgiven her and I still love her.

Not

We are troubled on every side, yet not distressed; we are perplexed, but not in despair; Persecuted, but not forsaken; cast down, but not destroyed. 2 Corinthians 4:8-9

One of my dear friends and I often got a chuckle out of her Dad's response to our inquiries of how he was doing. "How are you doing, Daddy," we'd ask. His standard response, "Bad." We were always amused by the fact that no matter what the circumstances, the weather or the physical condition he was in, he would always say, "Bad." And, this was the case, despite the fact that he was generally in a chipper mood. Similarly, my own Dad will at times give us commentary on his maladies. I once conversed with him about how I had been a bit under the weather. Before I could finish giving him the details of my illness, he interjected, "You weren't as sick as I was." I was so tickled by his statement and subsequent list of symptoms, that I forgot all about what ailed me. It seems everyone has his or her own brand of suffering. And it also seems that we sometimes tend to focus more on the negatives than the positives . . . the bad than the good . . . what we are rather than what we're not. Perhaps you've heard the trendy slang in which a statement is made, followed by the word, "not." For example, a person might say, "I think I'm going sell all of my shoes for a dollar . . . NOT." In this case the focus is more on the "not" than on the prior statement. The young people who fashioned this type of phrase may not have known how closely it resembles Paul's statement, found in II Corinthians. In it Paul is focusing more on the "nots" than the problems. He said we're surrounded by trouble, but we are *not* distressed, perplexed and confused but *not* in despair, bullied and tortured but *not* forsaken, thrown to the ground but *not* destroyed.

Here, what we *are not* is invariably more significant that what we *are*. The good news outweighs the bad news. And the word "not" takes on a new and promising meaning. "Not" turns out to be a not so bad word after all. When clouds of discouragement seem to overshadow you, flip the script and focus on what you're not. You may be down, but you're not out. You may be beaten up by the cares of life, but you're not defeated. You may be wounded but you're not dead. You may be sorrowful, but you're not without hope. And when the devil comes at you to berate and taunt you with evil threats of what he plans to heap upon you . . . your response should be . . . NOT.

Rabbi

And he said unto him, Why callest thou me good? There is none good but one, that is, God: but if thou wilt enter into life, keep the commandments. Matthew 19:17

Some people want to learn without being taught. Pride or other obstacles keep them from admitting there are some things they don't know. When Jesus walked the earth, He ran across more than a few such individuals. They challenged Him at every turn and debated with him. He was God and man, so of course they couldn't win the argument. But that didn't stop them from trying. And when they realized they couldn't outwit or out smart Him, they killed him. How's that for intellect and intelligence? And that is often the response to knowledge and truth when taught to people who want to learn, but don't want to be taught. They pointedly called Him "Good Master," a rarely used epithet for a Rabbi or teacher. They sarcastically even referred to Him as, "Rabbi." If they had only truly respected that title, they could have learned more in his few years on earth than in all the years it takes to acquire a PhD. And Jesus so wanted to teach them life lessons that would expand their way of thinking and enlighten their thought processes which had been retarded by arrogance and shallowness . . . a dangerous combination. They inquired of this "Good Master" how they might obtain life eternal. Before he answered them, He had a question of His own. "Why callest thou me good?" And Jesus' questions always shined a spotlight on the unwitting contestant. Much like on modern game shows where the one being quizzed is clueless to the right answer but takes a stab at the question anyway . . . the obnoxious buzzer signifying the fact that they are dead wrong. Chuck from Montana goes away with a useless parting gift, like two night's accommodations in a hotel in a city other than where he lives, and no plane tickets to get there. But when Jesus asked questions of his students, He at least sent them away with knowledge that would give them a shot at salvation. So on this day, He asked, "Why are you calling me good? There's only one who is good and that is God." Ding-Ding-Ding!! He snuck the answer in there on them. "I'm God! And if you obey the commandments and live like I'm attempting to teach you, you'll have eternal life." Quiz over . . . game over. So, calling Jesus good was the smartest thing they'd ever said. Pity it ended there for most. A little more time in His tutelage, seeking from Him wisdom and knowledge rather than seeking to prove Him wrong and seeking to take His life, and their lives would have been enhanced greatly. The world still has such attitudes lurking. We fear what we may learn if we actually spend time with Jesus and ask Him the right questions. We'd rather live based on what we believe we know. The threat of learning more and being responsible for more makes us seek to silence Him. Don't we know that learning the truths He offers will make us wise beyond mere knowledge . . . and make us more than scholars? And the wisdom and knowledge won't be a heavy burden, as some may think. It will empower us. That's why He still makes the invitation, "Take my yoke upon you and learn of me, for my yoke is easy and my burden is light." Jesus is teaching the same lessons today. Study. It will be the smartest thing you've ever done. And, there'll be an open book test at the end of the semester.

Henceforth ...

I have fought a good fight, I have finished my course, I have kept the faith: Henceforth there is laid up for me a crown of righteousness, which the Lord, the righteous judge, shall give me at that day and not to me only, but unto all them also that love his appearing. 2 Timothy 4:7-8

I once heard a preacher friend of mine say that the best way for us to endure the harsh trials of this life is for us to live in the "henceforth." He expounded on the fact that Paul was a prisoner and facing his impending death at the time of his second letter to Timothy. In this last will and testament, as it were, he stated that he was ready for whatever horrible fate awaited him because he was focused on the fact that henceforth . . . or in the future or time to come, there was a crown of righteousness laid up for him. And not just for him, but also for every person that is excited about and anticipating God's return. That includes you and me. Surely in this life, we will each have our share of trouble, grief, sorrow, and issues. But if we can look to the future, we can survive the present. After all, that's how Jesus endured the cross. *"Looking unto Jesus the author and finisher of our faith; who for the joy that was set before him endured the cross, despising the shame, and is set down at the right hand of the throne of God." (Hebrews 12:2)* If it worked for Jesus, the man, that's enough for me. Applying this practice to my own experience I have been able to get through dark days because of the hope of things to come. In the "henceforth," pain and suffering stops. In the "henceforth," broken hearts are mended. In the "henceforth," loved ones are reunited. Paul was on lock-down and had no real contact with the outside world. There was no escaping this prison and no hope of release. What could be more discouraging than that setting? Yet he writes these encouraging words, *"For God has not given us a spirit of fear;*

110

but of power, and of love and of a sound mind. Be not thou therefore ashamed of the testimony of our Lord, nor of me his prisoner but be thou partaker of the afflictions of the gospel according to the power of God." (2 Timothy 1:7-8) He was not afraid of what would soon happen to him. He knew a death sentence was at hand. *"For I am now ready to be offered, and the time of my departure is at hand." (V6)* Paul was, in fact, beheaded not long after he penned that letter to Timothy. What he was trying to convey was the fact that suffering and affliction are part of the Christian life. But there is another part of our experience that will sustain us, if we keep it in mind . . . the "henceforth." That's where after we've fought the good fight, kept the faith, and finished the sometimes-difficult course, we receive the crown of righteousness, to be handed to us by Jesus Christ himself. Paul may have been in a cell but he was thinking outside the box. And your circumstances may have you feeling as though you are imprisoned. If you'll think outside the scope of what you are going through and place yourself in the henceforth, you'll be amazed at what you can endure.

Natural Protection

*He that dwelleth in the secret place of the Most High shall
abide under the shadow of the almighty.*

Psalm 91:1

The world is a threatening place. All sorts of dangers lurk in the
shadows and lay in wait for us. Were we left to our own defenses, we
would merely be victims . . . the devil's prey. The Bible warns us that the
devil knows he has but a short time so he is as a roaring lion, seeking
whom he may devour. We are like tender meat for him. But God has
given us protection. I was talking to a newfound friend, Debi, who is an
expert on animals. In fact, she lives on a large horse ranch in Wyoming,
and comes in contact with animals in the wild on a daily basis. Our
family had the pleasure of conversing with her over dinner one day and
she shared with us the most fascinating stories of her encounters with
large herds of deer, bobcats, and mountain lions. In one interesting
account, she told us of the day she was riding a horse through a large
pasture. As the horse strode along slowly, she looked down and there
nestled in the tall grass, was a tiny, newborn deer. He was curled up in a
ball sleeping as his mother forged for food somewhere nearby. She told
us he was so little that she barely noticed him and probably wouldn't
have if she hadn't been seated so high on the horse. Of course we
ooed and aahed at the thought of this tender scene. Then she told us
that on the trail she had also noticed a mountain lion making his way
through the tall grass. I gasped, fearing for the fawn. But she informed
me that the baby deer was safe, because the young deer give off no
scent. They, in fact, have no scent until they mature. This, she said, is
their natural protection. Because they have no smell, their predators
cannot hunt them down by scent. I marveled at God. He gives the

young creatures a chance to mature before the enemy can hunt them down. That's what I would call "Supernatural Protection." God has given us certain defenses. He knows that the devil is seeking to devour us like a roaring lion. Sometimes He hides us from him, placing us in the tall grass where we can rest, secure. *He maketh me to lie down in green pastures . . . . Yeah tho I walk through the valley of the shadow of death, I will fear no evil. Thy rod and staff they comfort me."* (Psalm 23:2,4) While we have to keep our guard up against the enemy (watch and pray), it's comforting to know that God has given us natural and supernatural protection. Our natural protection is instinct and wisdom. And the supernatural protection takes up where human strengths leave off. Abide in the secret place that He has provided for you. His will is that secret place. And when the enemy comes to hunt for you as his prey, you can find safety under the wings of the Savior.

Under His Wings   . . . William O. Cushing
Under His wings, under His wings,
Who from His love can sever?
Under His wings my soul shall abide,
Safely abide forever.

What to do With Emptiness

Then he said, Go, borrow thee vessels abroad of all thy neighbours, even empty vessels; borrow not a few. ⁴ And when thou art come in, thou shalt shut the door upon thee and upon thy sons, and shalt pour out into all those vessels, and thou shalt set aside that which is full. ⁵ So she went from him, and shut the door upon her and upon her sons, who brought the vessels to her; and she poured out. ⁶ And it came to pass, when the vessels were full, that she said unto her son, Bring me yet a vessel. And he said unto her, There is not a vessel more. And the oil stayed. II Kings 3-6

Today's passage makes me aware of the fact that there is a benefit to emptiness. Certainly no one wants to be empty . . . to have run out of oil, so to speak. Emptiness is the opposite of what we spend our lives seeking . . . fullness. And we can fill our lives with things and still feel empty . . . void of anything meaningful. But emptiness can show promise. Sounds crazy, doesn't it? But it's true. The woman highlighted in this story had run out of everything. She was destitute and all she had left was her children . . . both of whom were about to be taken away to satisfy a debt, and she had a little oil. I'd say she was empty. When the prophet Elisha came and asked her what he could do for her, she poured out her sad story telling him that, Oy Vey, all she has left in her house is this little bit of cooking oil. His response is very interesting and gives hope by its very nature. He didn't tell her to try to go and borrow oil from neighbors. He didn't tell her to try to borrow money. He told her to go and get empty pots. To me this signifies that there is a benefit to emptiness. The benefit is that where there is emptiness, there is potential and we can be filled. In our emptiness, God has the opportunity to fill us to the brim. So she rounds up all these empty vessels and closes herself off with her family, and begins to pour out what little she has into these empty pots. And she runs out of pots before she runs out of oil! When the empty pots were full, we know there was still oil in her bottle because she asked her sons to bring her another pot and there were no more to fill. Emptiness proved to be a blessing to her. And that same emptiness can be a blessing for us too. For in it, God shows His ability and willingness to fill us up! The problem is we won't bring him our emptiness. We try to fill ourselves and if we do happen to bring him our empty vessels, we're ashamed to show just how empty we are so we bring the small empty vessels and leave the big 50-gallon tank of emptiness hidden somewhere. We go away still half empty because we didn't bring enough emptiness for Him to fill. We do the same thing with the blessings that God is offering us. Here we stand in the very presence of the fountain of Living Water, with a teacup. (Pinky extended.) We're trying to be dainty when we're EMPTY. God is offering to fill up our emptiness and we're politely brushing Him off, pretending we're full. We should be dragging every empty vessel we can find to the filling station and screaming, fill 'er up! (In our best trucker voice.) If the prophet Elisha were to tell me to go and get some vessels to be filled, I'd be on the phone with Shell Oil Company trying to borrow or lease a tanker truck. I'd back that thing up and my daughter Brooke and I would pour my Crisco—I'm sorry, Canola oil in until it overflowed. I realize that I need to be filled and I'm not ashamed to say it. We need to stop trying to be cute and tell God that we are EMPTY and need for Him to fill us up! That's what you do with emptiness. You allow God to fill it. When we attempt to fill ourselves, we wind up full of things that do not satisfy. Though full, we still feel empty. Confess to God today that you are running on empty and need the oil of joy, peace, hope, faith, mercy, and every other good thing that cannot be purchased in the grocery store. Most of all, I want to be Spirit filled. Bring Him your emptiness.

Rags to Riches

I will greatly rejoice in the LORD, my soul shall be joyful in my God; for he hath clothed me with the garments of salvation, he hath covered me with the robe of righteousness, as a bridegroom decketh himself with ornaments, and as a bride adorneth herself with her jewels. Isaiah 61:10

Sometimes a tattered and torn life can make you feel so unworthy and out of sorts. It's like showing up at an elegant ball, dressed in your tattered, chore clothing. Everyone else seems dressed for the occasion, as if they got the memo. You, on the other hand, were left out of the loop and so you arrived in your torn, cut-off, jean shorts with the frayed edges, your "old-faithful" T-shirt . . . you know the one with the paint stains on it from when you redecorated the den, and flip-flops. You glance down and realize how badly in need of a pedicure you are. And now, all eyes are on you because you just don't fit in with the decorum or the dress code. You stand out like white clothes after Labor Day. As struggling Christians, we often feel that way. It appears that everyone else is well suited for the "event" of Christianity. Yet, here we are underdressed or even undressed. Our mistake fraught lives have left us feeling naked and all we're wearing is the scars and stretch marks of sin. And they don't exactly make for impressive attire. The truth is everyone has those scars. Read it in His book, *"As it is written, There is none righteous, no, not one." (Romans 3:10)* That's right. Despite the earthly designer clothing or tailoring, underneath everyone is wearing rags. It is the righteousness of God, when placed over our nakedness or unsightly undergarments, which outfits us for the big event. Now, of course we would do well to make an earnest attempt to put on something appropriate, like the breastplate of salvation. My mother used to warn us to always wear good underwear just in case we got in an accident, as if it would matter to the Emergency Room attendants or us, the unconscious victim. Can't you just see it? The hurried treatment of the medical team stops abruptly with a collective gasp at the sight of your faded briefs. Unlikely. But God doesn't want shame to be our clothing. Jesus is the best wardrobe coordinator and He knows what is suitable for you to wear as you attempt to dress for success. You may not always be the best dressed, and your clothing from the past may leave you feeling a bit embarrassed, but God's grace is the most appropriate apparel you can wear. I realize that even in my best efforts to live the life, talk the talk, and walk the walk, I still need the grace of God to cover me and make me feel less ashamed of the scars, the ill-fitted garments of foolishness or the ragged clothing of sin. I relish in what the prophet Isaiah heralds, embracing it as my own testimony . . . that I will "greatly rejoice in the Lord and my soul shall be joyful in my God because He has clothed me with the garments of salvation and covered me with the robe of righteousness." I'm outfitted in attire that will never be out of fashion, out of place or outdated. My designer is the Creator.

Anesthesia

For the heart of this people is waxed gross, and their ears are dull of hearing, and their eyes have they closed; lest they should see with their eyes, and hear with their ears, and understand with their heart, and should be converted, and I should heal them. Acts 28:27

Anyone who has ever had surgery can attest to the fact that anesthesia is a powerful thing. Typically before the surgical procedure is begun, the medical staff will administer this drug and the patient is then told to count backwards from ten. Most often the last thing the patient remembers is saying the word "ten" . . . or maybe "nine". You feel no pain or discomfort even though you are being cut and carved and sometimes undergoing a harsh and aggressive procedure. You feel nothing. The anesthetic potency of the drug has numbed you to the pain of the situation. Once the operation is over, the patient is gently awakened and then given strong pain medications to further anesthetize them to the discomforts of what they have been through. There have been times in my life when I have self-medicated, figuratively. I scheduled myself, as it were, to undergo a harsh and invasive procedure. I guess you could call it "elective," because I chose to go through what I went through despite the fact I knew it would be brutal. In order to pursue my course, I had to numb myself to the reality. Many are in the same condition. In a state of unconsciousness or under anesthesia in a spiritual sense. We don't want to face up to what is actually going on in our lives or experience the painful reality of our actions because then we'd be forced to acknowledge them and maybe even do something about it. Our hearts are hardened, our ears plugged with cotton, our eyes closed to keep us from seeing, hearing and understanding what is necessary for our conversion. Consequently, at the end of the self-performed procedure, we never heal. The anesthesia keeps us just numb enough to continue the covert operation, lest we be converted. How do we break the cycle? How do we change something that, despite its harmful nature, is what we desire? If I were to write, "I don't know" here, you would go away disappointed and perhaps even irritated by the fact that no answer had been given. Well, the truth is, I don't know the perfect answer for how to break the cycle and change. But I do know that God has that perfect answer. And it starts by first acknowledging that you are under the influence of something so powerful that it is placing you in a state of unconsciousness. Once willing to make that admission, God can begin the work of waking us out of our induced sleep. A sleep, induced by alcohol, fantasy, denial, false justification, pride or whatever our anesthesia of choice. Being numb to the truth yields a slow self-destruction. Today, we ask God to open our hearts, ears, and eyes, then nudge us gently and whisper . . . "It's time to wake up." The surgical procedure is over and it's time for conversion and healing. Warning: Once awake, the patient may need to spend some time in recovery.

Promises, Promises

For all the promises of God in him are yea, and in him Amen, unto the glory of God by us.

II Corinthians 1:20

When I make a promise, I try very hard to keep it. Especially when it comes to promises made to children. One of the worst offenses a person can make, in my opinion, is to break a promise to a child because of how trusting they are and how fragile their hope can be. Although I'm reluctant to make promises for fear of failure, I'm powerless when children, like my daughter, ask me to promise to do something. I would imagine it's because they are so adorable and innocent and I absolutely love children. God has made quite a lot of promises to us in His Word. And He is faithful to honor them, each and every one. I wonder if His reasoning for making and keeping promises to us is the same as mine. We certainly aren't innocent, but we are His children. And maybe, just maybe, we are adorable to Him. It's okay to blush here. One thing is for certain . . . He loves us. And so He makes a wealth of promises to us and some of them are really big ones. What's even more wonderful is that He never breaks His promises. He's made these huge promises to His children throughout history. One of my favorites is the one made to the Children of Israel. He said, *"Every place whereon the soles of your feet shall tread shall be yours: from the wilderness and Lebanon, from the river, the river Euphrates, even unto the uttermost sea shall your coast be. There shall no man be able to stand before you: for the Lord your God shall lay the fear of you and the dread of you upon all the land that ye shall tread upon, as he hath said unto you."* (Deuteronomy 11:24-25) Big promise, and He kept it. He's promised us the same wealth of blessings. When it seems that the promises that God has made us aren't coming to pass in our lives, we may need to consider whether we have held up our end of the promise. Have we been obedient children? Have we met the conditions by which the blessings can be experienced? *"Behold, I set before you this day a blessing and a curse; A blessing, if ye obey the commandments of the LORD your God, which I command you this day: And a curse, if ye will not obey the commandments of the LORD your God, but turn aside out of the way which I command you this day, to go after other gods, which ye have not known."* *(Verses 26-28)* God wants to bless us and provide for us every good and perfect gift. He has promised that no good thing will He withhold from them that walk uprightly. (Ps. 84:11) But we must do our part to see the promise fulfilled. God's promises and covenants are sound and sincere. We can count on them. What promises have we made to Him? So often our promises come as a result of some difficulty we are facing or trouble in which we find ourselves. The commitments begin something like this, "Lord if you will get me out of this situation, I will . . ." And you can fill in the blanks. When God comes through, which He often does, we sometimes forget our promise. Yet we expect God to keep every promise He's made to us . . . and He does, because He doesn't make empty promises, better known as lies. *"God is not a man, that he should lie; neither the son of man, that he should repent: hath he said, and shall he not do it? Or hath he spoken, and shall he not make it good?"* *(Numbers 23:19)* However, in a loving relationship, promises are reciprocal. Those in such relationships delight to do loving things for each other. In our relationship with God we should carry out the same practices. Our promises shouldn't be the result of need, but love. After all, that's what His promises are based on. And the promises we've made to Him should be kept. If there is a commitment you've made to God and not kept, today would be a good day to begin your effort to live up to it. No doubt there are promises from His Word that you are clinging to. You needn't worry about whether He will come through. Will you?

Be Who You Are...

". . . For he maketh his sun to rise on the evil and on the good, and sendeth rain on the just and on the unjust." Matthew 5:45

Why is it that we so often let people change us? Their actions sometimes prompt us to change who we are. People hurt us; we become less trusting. We feel taken advantage of, so we become less giving. People mistreat us, so we decide we aren't going to be as kind to others anymore. I have long held to the belief that we shouldn't allow other people's actions to dictate our own. That is until one day I started to feel unappreciated and taken for granted. I became irritated by the fact that the things I had done for others had been ignored and overlooked. Oddly, this was only days after I had been encouraging a sister of mine who was questioning whether she had been too generous with someone. I told her that she shouldn't feel guilty for being who she was . . . a loving individual who liked to make others happy. And now, here I was venting to a friend about my own hurt feelings and angrily informing him that I was done doing kind things for people who didn't deserve them. In a very calm voice he reminded me of a fact that would have further irritated me, had he not been correct and had I not recognized his words as the loving counsel of a true friend. He asked me the rhetorical question, "Does God refuse to rain on us because we don't deserve it?" He went on, "What if God decided to never rain on us again because we didn't deserve the rain?" By now I had the point, but he didn't stop. "Flowers don't bloom because we deserve to see their colors . . . they bloom because they are flowers. You don't do the kind things you do because people deserve them . . . you do them because you are a kind person . . . a flower. Don't stop blooming because you feel people don't deserve it.

Be who you are. God doesn't rain on us because we deserve to have water. He rains on us because He's God." I replayed his sermonette in my mind several more times, letting it sink in. I was actually relieved that I didn't have to attempt to follow through with my angry, vain, and idle threat to stop being so nice to others. His words freed me and gave me permission to go on doing unto others, as I would have them do unto me . . . even if they don't ascribe to the same philosophy. And so I offer the same words of counsel to you. If you are the type of person who is giving and optimistic, don't allow the misguided actions or reactions of others to drive out your Christ-like characteristics. God doesn't rain on us because we deserve it. He rains on us because He's God. Follow His example. This doesn't mean you should allow yourself to be taken advantage of or used, but you should allow yourself to be used by the Lord and maintain an attitude of kindness. I know that I have done nothing to deserve the immense kindness and mercy that God has bestowed upon me. His loving kindness is better than life to me. (Psalm 63:3) And His mercy seems limitless . . . the Word says it endureth forever. (Psalm 106:1) My actions have not always reflected my gratitude and appreciation, however my rudeness has not changed Who He is. He remains a loving God, in spite of me. I wonder if I can possess and reveal the same qualities in my life? Is it humanly possible? Even if I don't think it's humanly possible given who I am . . . I know that it's supernaturally possible. I can do all things through Christ, which strengthens me. (Philippians 4:13)

Preparation

"Lo, I am coming like a thief! Blessed is he who is awake, keeping his garments that he may not go naked and be seen exposed!"
Revelation 16:15

A very common recurring nightmare is the one where the person is standing before an audience without any clothes or in some public place wearing nothing but a larger version of the suit given to them at birth. What evokes this recurring nightmare may vary, but generally relates to the fear of inadequacy or exposure. I have a recurring nightmare where I am standing in a pulpit before a large crowd of people and I have no sermon. Just as I get ready to speak, I realize that I didn't bring my notes. Essentially, I'm unprepared. The horror. I pray that the nightmare will never play out in real life, but I understand that I have to make every effort to be prepared in order to decrease the degree of likeliness. The thought of being unprepared is a frightful one. No one wants to walk into an interview unprepared. If tax time sneaks up on us before we've had a chance to get our taxes prepared, thoughts of the IRS knocking on our doors with handcuffs start to dance in our heads. And how many have been surprised by more dinner guests than they had planned for? It's just not a comfortable thing. I have a friend who was planning to take on a very important singing engagement. Although the invitation was flattering, he was fretful of being unprepared. So he practiced day and night until he was practically coughing out notes. He just didn't want to be unprepared and experience a real life version of the recurring nightmare of standing on a stage before thousands in his underwear. Being ready brings peace. The problem is, some tend to put things off until it's too late and then they attempt, unsuccessfully, to prepare in haste what should have been planned for well in advance. The return of the Lord will be no different. Like tax season, we know it's coming. We can work each day to be sure that we are not caught unaware. Or we can let the day sneak up on us with catastrophic results. I was a terrible college student. Were it not for friends who nagged and nudged me to study and go to class, I would probably still be sitting in a classroom at Oakwood University now, wondering why all the students looked so much younger than me. My problem was procrastination. I always thought I had more time than I actually had. I would put off reading chapters and then attempt to speed-read through them the night before a test. Did I mention I wasn't a speed-reader? And, since learning by sleeping with a book under your pillow doesn't really work, you have an idea of how my grades sometimes looked. I guess you could say I was testing the theory of osmosis. I had to eventually study, participate, and practice. Being ready for the return of the Lord requires the same. We have to study, to participate in the work of salvation, and adopt the right practices. Anything less will leave us naked. Although God created me and knows what my dark clothing is hiding, I still don't want to stand naked before Him. We're admonished to watch and pray. We have to be awake to do this. If we allow His coming to catch us unprepared, then the shame really is on us because it's not as if we didn't know it was on the horizon. We may not know exactly when, but we do know the Lord is coming. We don't have to let His return be nightmarish. *Matthew 24:44—Therefore you also must be ready; for the Son of man is coming at an hour you do not expect.*

Near Life Experiences

I am come that they might have life, and that they might have it more abundantly. John 10:10

You've probably heard accounts of people who've had what they believe to have been "near death" experiences. They describe it as peaceful and painless and some say they saw a bright light at the end of a tunnel. I've never had a so-called "near death" experience that I know of, but I can say that I have had a few "near life" experiences. These are what I would describe as times when I too saw a light at the end of the tunnel and had I elected to follow that light I would have experienced life more abundantly. Had I studied a little longer, had I sought the Lord more diligently, had I taken a right instead of a left, moved North instead of South, tried saving instead of spending . . . . In each of those instances, life would have been different, better, happier. And in reminiscing on my "near life" experiences, I wished I didn't have to "come back". But perhaps, like those who claim to have seen the light and heard a voice telling them it wasn't their time, it may not have been my time. Maybe, just maybe, the way my life is now is the way it was meant to be. Even with the regrets, and the recriminations, isn't it possible that God allowed me to experience just what I am experiencing now so that I might reach His intended end? Certainly each of us has our own idea of how our lives should have been or should be, but if we connect ourselves to Christ, follow His light, and seek His will, we won't have "near life" experiences, but we will live abundantly. What *could have been* is of no consequence. What actually is, is what's most important. Christ came into the world to give you life . . . THAT'S the light at the end of the tunnel. Walk toward it. Walk in it, and live in it. Here's what happens when you do, life's events become more bearable because you're living in the light. No more merely existing in a dark tunnel of despair. *Ephesians 5:8—For ye were sometimes darkness, but now are ye light in the Lord: walk as children of light.* Not enough light for you? You have been called to live as a chosen and special individual. *1 Peter 2:9* puts it this way . . . *But ye are a chosen generation, a royal priesthood, an holy nation, a peculiar people; that ye should show forth the praises of him who hath called you out of darkness into his marvelous light!* Live in it!

Perspective

For I was hungry and you gave me nothing to eat, I was thirsty and you gave me nothing to drink, I was a stranger and you did not invite me in, I needed clothes and you did not clothe me, I was sick and in prison and you did not look after me. They also will answer, 'Lord, when did we see you hungry or thirsty or a stranger or needing clothes or sick or in prison, and did not help you?' "He will reply, 'I tell you the truth, whatever you did not do for one of the least of these, you did not do for me.' Matthew 25:42-45

It was a cold and rainy evening, 3 days before Thanksgiving, and as I stood outside the closed hair salon waiting for my hairdresser to arrive, I commiserated with myself about my misfortune. I was cold, slightly damp, and irritated by the fact that the stylist was late and I had to stand outside waiting for him. Just when I was about to make a really good point to myself in my complaint, a woman walked up to me and interrupted my self-pity party. This woman was soaked through from head to toe and had obviously been walking around in the pouring rain all day. She was drenched and, compared to her, I was dry as I stood underneath the awning. As she approached me I could see that she was cold and apparently homeless because she carried a bag filled with what were probably her belongings. She stepped closer and stopped in front of me, "Ma'am, would you be willing to buy me a sandwich? I'm very hungry and I have no money. If you could just give me a dollar I'll come back and show you the burger." I told her, "Sweetheart, I would be happy to give you money to buy something to eat, and you don't have to come and show me anything. In this life we are on the honor system." As I looked through my purse, I realized that I had no cash. So I offered to walk with her to the nearby McDonald's and buy her a meal. She seemed stunned by my willingness, but off we walked in the rain together. Inside the restaurant I stepped up to the counter with her and told her to order anything she wanted. "Can I get a double cheese-burger?" "Of course," I said, "get anything you want." She looked back at me and asked, "May I have some French fries?" This request nearly broke my heart. "Yes! By all means, get whatever you'd like. Get a soda too." She refused the soda and a cookie I offered to buy, telling me that she would drink water because she didn't want to spend too much of my money. I swiped my debit card to pay for the food feeling sad and crushed. As she left with her bag of food, she looked at me and said, thank you. I said, "God bless you," and she responded, "He already has, through you." By now I was fighting back tears. The fight ended as I watched her walking down the street in the rain, eating her dinner from a wet paper bag. My how this experience put things in perspective for me. Here I was complaining about standing outside for a few minutes and having to wait to get my hair done, when another woman about my same age was trying to figure out where her next meal would come from. When our worlds intersected for that brief moment in time, she changed my outlook, showing me the flip side of life. I was ashamed. How ungrateful we must seem to God at times. We enjoy such luxuries, and still we complain. He more than meets our needs, and our wants increase. Meanwhile in the distance a person stands in the cold rain, not only wanting, but *needing*. What a privilege to be the hands that God can use to meet the needs of even one. And while that woman may not know it, she impacted me more, I'm sure, than I impacted her. The food may have filled her stomach, but she filled my soul. And as her hunger was satisfied, so too was mine. My hunger for more. My selfishness subsided and my wait in the rain became less bothersome. Who knew that McDonald's served humble pie?

Living by the Rules

. . . Thou hast given commandment to save me . . . Psalms 71:3

Many people get all hung up in the commandments and therefore miss out on a loving relationship with God. I've heard it said on more than one occasion, "Religion has too many rules and restrictions." This is usually uttered by those who have had less than pleasant church experiences and who haven't had the opportunity to understand the relationship aspect of our experience with God. The commandments are not meant to simply be strict, but to save. God is trying to spare us the pain of the consequences of sin. If we err, He is faithful to forgive . . . yet the consequences of our actions often have to be experienced. That's what He's trying to prevent us from having to endure. Countless times my parents tried to counsel me against doing something foolish, which they knew would render consequences that would be uncomfortable at best and destructive at worst. They set up rules for my siblings and me, which seemed strict and arduous. We complained, silently—not wanting to evoke the wrath of my mother and her terrible swift sword, but complied, in most cases. When we did obey, I don't know if we realized at the time what pain we had been spared. But as I look back, I can clearly see why they imposed the rules. I'm sure my daughter is now suffering from the same blindness to the need for rules that I suffered at her age. However, as I reflect on my childhood, I understand why we were not allowed to spend the night at the homes of any and all friends. My mother didn't allow many sleepovers. Her refusal often angered me, especially when I saw many of my other friends being allowed. But she had her reasons. Now taking into consideration the dangers of child molestation and other evils, I can't say I blame her. In fact, I thank her. We had to be home at a certain time. The curfew was not meant to oppress, but to protect. My parents believed nothing good was happening out on the streets after 11:00 at night. They were right. My brother Bobby disputed that fact, until he came in one night incoherent and confused, his so-called friends having drugged him. A trip to the hospital, with a nearly hysterical mother and father, to have his stomach pumped, confirmed the fact that my parents were right. Yet and still it wasn't a lesson easily learned for him. The fact of the matter is that rules often spark in human nature the urge to rebel against them. And the element of love doesn't always alter our reaction to rules. But maturity and respect should. God's rules are not the marching orders of some cruel and harsh tyrant who wants to control us. They are the instructions of a loving parent intent on protecting us from ridiculous outcomes. He offers them in love to help us. If we will focus more on the love and less on the restrictions, how much easier it will be to comprehend and obey. When we obey and follow His commands, we enjoy the peace of knowing that we don't have to really fear the outcome. Even if unfortunate circumstances befall us, we know that it is through no fault of our own. The rules are for our own good. When I have followed them, I have been free to relax without looking over my shoulder, waiting for the other shoe to drop, fearing being found out or cleaning up the mess I've made. Do you love Him? If your answer is 'yes' then follow the rules of a loving Father. *If you love me, keep my commandments.* (John 14:15) They carry far less regret than the consequences of failing to follow them. Look at it this way, it's not so much what we can't do, but more what we can do. Not so much what we aren't allowed to do, but more what we are allowed to do. I wasn't allowed to stay out after 11:00, but I was allowed to come to a safe home, get a good night's sleep and avoid arrest along with my friends who got into trouble later that night. I'm not allowed to steal, but I am allowed to earn what I want to obtain, work for it and again avoid arrest. Not breaking the rules brings peace and spares us the risk of punishment . . . not from God, but from consequences. That's what He wants for each of us.

Red Sea Miracles

*And Moses stretched out his hand over the sea; and the LORD caused
the sea to go back by a strong east wind all that night, and made the
sea dry land, and the waters were divided. And the children of Israel
went into the midst of the sea upon the dry ground: and the waters
were a wall unto them on their right hand, and on their left. And the
Egyptians pursued, and went in after them to the midst of the sea, even
all Pharaoh's horses, his chariots, and his horsemen. And the LORD
said unto Moses, Stretch out thine hand over the sea, that the waters
may come again upon the Egyptians, upon their chariots, and upon
their horsemen. And Moses stretched forth his hand over the sea, and
the sea returned to his strength when the morning appeared; and the
Egyptians fled against it; and the LORD overthrew the Egyptians in
the midst of the sea. And the waters returned, and covered the chariots,
and the horsemen, and all the host of Pharaoh that came into the sea
after them; there remained not so much as one of them.*

Exodus 14:21-23, 26-28

We don't always realize it, but everyday that we wake up in the
morning we are experiencing a miracle. With all of the dark forces
that are working against us and the plot of the enemy to destroy us,
life itself is a miraculous occurrence. That is a miracle that we should
never take for granted . . . a large one at that. Small miracles are
wonderful . . . you know like when the car makes it a few extra miles
when you know you should have run out of gas? But there are times
we need large miracles . . . Red Sea miracles. When the freed Hebrew
slaves made their exodus from Egyptian captivity with Pharaoh and
his bloodthirsty army in pursuit, they needed more than the miracle
of good weather for their travels. A working navigation system and

low-priced gas weren't exactly what they were interested in enjoying. They needed something big . . . like the parting of a sea so they could walk through on dry land, escaping death or, worse yet, a return to slavery. Technically, I guess you could say there is no such thing as a small miracle if God is providing something that you needed and had no power to produce. Considering that, yes, I appreciate the miracle of leaving late and still getting my daughter to school on time. In those instances God indeed has parted the traffic on I-5 and allowed me us to win the race against time. But there are times when what we need are Red Sea, raising Lazarus from the dead, healing the 12-year issue of blood, feeding the multitude of 5 thousand with 5 loaves and 2 fish, turning water into wine, restoring sight to the blind miracles. And this is when I rejoice knowing there is no miracle too great for God to be able to perform in our lives. Great problems call for great miracles, just as desperate times require desperate measures. And God has proven that He's willing to go to those measures on our behalf. As you are reading this, your spirit is being lifted because right now you're up against a major problem and what you need is a Red Sea miracle. Your circumstances are critical and you need a Red Sea miracle. God is still in the Red Sea miracle business. He's the God of your salvation and a major miracle is in His hand and within your grasp. When you wake up tomorrow morning thank Him for the everyday miracle, but don't be afraid to ask Him to open the Red Sea. He did it before, and He can and will do it again . . . for you.

The Cover-up

Blessed is he whose transgression is forgiven, whose sin is covered.
Blessed is the man unto whom the Lord imputeth not iniquity,
and in whose spirit there is no guile. Psalm 32:1-2

Today's text is one of my favorites. I envision a loving parent going to the children's rooms in the wee hours of the morning, covering their sleeping children to protect them from the drafts and cold. I have enjoyed the benefits of such cover-ups during my lifetime. And truly it is a blessing to be covered from the coldness of the world and the ridicule that often comes with just living. We make mistakes that leave us exposed. We commit acts that leave us feeling naked. And today's passage reassures us that with repentance, God acts as that loving parent who covers us up so that we won't be affected by the coldness or the draft of society, the church, friends or the public. Truly blessed is the man whose sin is covered. He wants to spare us embarrassment and shame. One ingredient that must be part of the equation, however, is a heart that is filled with no guile or deceit. In other words, we have to be contrite and humble before Him. We have to allow Him to cover us. If we belligerently continue to throw back the covers, exposing ourselves time and time again or, with an attitude of arrogant entitlement, presume that He will hide our sin, we'd better get ready for the dunce cap. He does not desire that our wrongs be put on public display, because He loves us so much that He wants to preserve our integrity. But there has to be some existing integrity to be preserved. I've made my share of mistakes, none of which I am proud or wish to see played on the big screen. But I take comfort in knowing that my loving Heavenly Father is just as interested in keeping them from being a box office hit. I'm not eager to see the motion picture,

"Scandal . . . starring Linda Anderson." This means I have to strive not to star in the film in the first place. But for past performances, for which I have asked forgiveness and changed my course and life, I celebrate the cover-up that my Father, through Jesus Christ, has performed. In the time of trouble, He has promised that He will hide us. When poor choices have placed us in embarrassing situations, with repentance God can and often will hide us from the troublesome outcome. Certainly there will be consequences for our actions, but God will buffer the blow. And if we are smart enough to repent—which means change—before the consequences lead to exposure, God, in His mercy, will often cover us. He does this not only to spare *us*, but those who are watching and might be led astray or broken by our open-faced indiscretion. Here's an idea. Turn, today, from whatever you are doing that will lead to eventual embarrassment or even disaster. Confess your need for forgiveness to God and then allow Him to cover you. (I John 1:9) His love is the warm throw of protection. Imagine how the woman caught in the very act of adultery must have felt as she heard the stones dropping to the ground from the hands of her accusers that day. I think that's one of the best sounds ever heard . . . the sound of rocks being dropped . . . but think how wonderful it also felt to have Jesus stoop down with a robe to cover her and hide her sin and shame, protecting her from the cold looks and the draft of the world. It was a robe of righteousness that allowed her to go and sin no more so that she might take pleasure in the cover-up.

The Blow of Salvation

Make haste to help me, O Lord my salvation. Psalm 38:22

We had an electric teapot that we kept on the kitchen counter. Everyone in the family used it to make hot beverages. This was in the pre-microwave era, so I'm dating myself, but I couldn't have been more than 12 or 13 years old. I had used this electric kettle countless times but this time stands out in my mind. On this particular morning, I was standing by the counter making my favorite hot drink in the teapot. I wasn't aware that the counter, which had a metal strip all the way around it, was wet. As I stirred my Postum in the pot, with a metal spoon, the spoon touched the bottom of the metal pot. Now this might not have presented a problem had it not been for the fact that I had my other hand on the wet metal of the wet counter. Yes, now you see where I'm going. Instant conductor. The electricity arced . . . in me. I stood there, frozen, spoon still touching the bottom of the plugged in pot with my right hand . . . left hand involuntarily gripped to the wet counter. I was being electrocuted and I couldn't do a thing about it. I was powerless to stop this action. My father just happened to be in the kitchen and looked up and noticed his youngest daughter, the lightening rod, receiving shock treatment at the kitchen counter. I don't know what it was that prompted him to look at me. Maybe it was the flickering of the lights or the faint squealing sound I may have been making. But he looked up and sprang into action. He ran across the room and, with all his might, slugged me in the shoulder. He couldn't touch or grab me because the charge then would have connected with him and we both would have been fried. But when he punched me, he broke the charge. The spoon flew out of my hand, I collapsed and he caught me. I don't have much recollection of what happened after that, other than the fact that my joints ached for days. But other than that, I sustained no major injuries, although some might say that I was brain damaged. Praise God that my father had his eyes on me. He noticed that I was in trouble and in order to save me, he struck me. (God is our refuge and strength; a very present help in trouble. Psalm 5:8) My father saw me in serious trouble. He had to break the grip of death and a blow was the only way to do it. And sometimes our Heavenly Father has to save us in the same manner. He sees us frozen in the grip of sin, evil, death . . . and He strikes us with a blow to save us. It's a loving blow, but a blow nonetheless. Remember Saul's blow on the road to Damascus, which brought about the salvation of Paul. (Acts 9) That's the way our Father has to rescue us at times. Recognizing the urgency He acts swiftly and decisively. If you saw your child standing in the path of an oncoming 18-wheeler, you wouldn't quietly announce in your best baby voice, "Snookums, there's a big, mean truck coming toward you at a really high rate of speed. If it makes contact with mommy's little sweetie-pie that's not going to be a nice thingy-wingy, so do mommy a favor and skip out of the road, Pumpkin." You would reach out and yank your child to safety, even if you wound up dislocating his or her shoulder in the process. The desire to save sometimes requires harsh, and painful measures. Yes, sometimes God has to hurt us to help us. His loving blow, however, is far less damaging than the outcome without His intervention. I'm thankful for the punch from my father that saved my life. I'm learning to be thankful for the blows from the Father that save my soul. Oh, and, by the way, we threw out that teapot.

Strawberry Pie

*And I will pray the Father, and he shall give you another Comforter,
that he may abide with you for ever; Even the Spirit of truth; whom
the world cannot receive, because it seeth him not, neither knoweth
him: but ye know him; for he dwelleth with you, and shall be in you.
I will not leave you comfortless: I will come to you. John 14:16-18*

The phone rang, waking me out of a deep sleep and interrupting
a dream I wasn't particularly enjoying. I fumbled for the phone. It was
1:10 a.m. Anyone calling at this hour either had a wrong number or
bad news. I feared it was the latter. I was right. My friend Lisa's sleepy
voice spoke softly what my heart heard loudly, "Rette's mom passed."
Loretta, affectionately knows as "Rette", to us, was part of what you
might call our 'best friend quartet' from college. The four of us, Lisa,
Loretta, Gina and I had been best friends for nearly 30 years. We were
so close that one of our Bible professors named us the "L Sisters." Gina
was an honorary member even though her name didn't start with
an "L". "Gina just called," she continued. "She'll call us back in the
morning, but she wanted us to know." We sighed, said our goodnights
and hung up. I slid out of bed onto my knees to speak to God about
what my friend, Rette, must be going through at that very hour and
what she would experience over the next few days, weeks, and months.
Less than 24 hours earlier, I was on the phone with Rette talking about
what lay ahead for her, as her precious mother's life ebbed. Having
lost my mother, she asked what she should expect. I shared what I
could, but informed her of what she already knew . . . that nothing can
prepare you for such loss. As we talked at 5:00 that previous morning,
we reminisced about her mother's strength and determination. Rette
showed the same strength. She trusted God and was holding onto

the hope of salvation for her mother. Still, sadness hung in the air. In a feeble attempt to lighten each other's spirits, we joked about her mom's strength of will. She had been a Civil Rights activists in her youth. Rette's mom had quite a lot of attributes. Her baking was one. She made the best strawberry pie in the world and would often ship them to us when we were roommates in college. We would sit, huddled in our dorm room, quietly eating the pie so as not to have to share it with anyone. It suddenly occurred to me that we might never enjoy her pie again and with that, I blurted out, "Rette, please tell me you have the recipe for Mom's strawberry pie! You didn't fall down on the job, did you?!" We both laughed, and she responded, "Yes, I have the recipe for the filling, but I was worried because I didn't have the recipe for her crust. But, thank goodness, my cousin Debbie told me that she has it. So I'll be making Mom's strawberry pie for Christmas." I wanted to cry, but I was still in "cheer Loretta mode." My friend didn't realize it, but she had just preached a sermon to me, that had encouraged *me*. It wasn't just about her mother's delicious pie, but the faithfulness of God. He used the strawberry pie to illustrate it. The lesson is this. Even when we don't have everything we need to make life whole, God gives us the missing ingredients to complete the blessing. He doesn't leave us with only part of the recipe for joy, but He sometimes sends others to compensate for what we lack. Like friends and loved ones who stand in the gap, and the Holy Spirit. He puts it like this; "I will not leave you comfortless . . ." The Holy Spirit would be both mother and father now. That's what I call comfort food. God had made provision for my friend in her time of sorrow. She had the filling, He provided the crust. Oh taste and see that the Lord is good!

Help

God is our refuge and strength; a very present help in trouble.
Psalm 46:1

The end of my workday stirred up a silent celebration in my spirit. I was tired and welcomed the thought of going home to my daughter and niece to enjoy a quiet night of relaxation. As I made my way out of the office parking lot, I saw a woman parked precariously at the entrance, the rear of her car nearly in the roadway. She was talking on a cell phone and she had a small child in the passenger seat. A fleeting thought said, "Just mind your business and go home, Linda." But, that not being my nature, I let down my window and asked the woman if she was alright. She quickly responded, "No." I then asked if she needed help and this response came just as quickly as the first, "Yes." In that short answer was contained her relief and gratitude that someone bothered to offer her assistance. She informed me that the car had stalled in the road but she had managed to coast to where it now sat. I parked my own car and got out, as if I knew anything about cars. "Try starting it again, without pressing the gas," I suggested. "You don't want to flood it." My words rang like a true mechanic. So much so that she stepped aside and asked me to give it a try. I got in and turned the key several times, but, sure enough, the car was not starting. That being the extent of my auto expertise, my next idea was that we push it into the parking lot and call a real mechanic. Just then a co-worker of mine drove up in her car. I beckoned her and asked if she could help us push. She agreed and the three of us attempted to push this SUV while I steered. I'm sure it's no surprise that the car didn't budge even one inch. We meant well, but we didn't have the strength. Next, another gentleman colleague pulled up . . . an ex-football player. He jumped behind the car and put his strength into it. The car began to budge and moved slowly. A group of men in a passing van noticed our plight. They pulled over and two joined us in operation push. Now the car moved with greater ease up the incline. As the pace quickened one gentleman told me to jump in. Running alongside the car, barefoot and in a dress, I hopped in and steered it into a parking slot. Mission accomplished. The group of helpers dispersed. I hugged this stranger and asked if she would be all right. She assured me she would because a friend was on his way to help her get the car to a repair shop. As I drove home reflecting on the incident, it unfolded like a step-by-step "how to" guide for getting help. You see, sometimes we don't seek help until we are at a standstill . . . dead end. When everything stops and we're at the point of desperation, we are ready to admit that we need help and actually welcome it. "Are you alright?" "No." "Do you need help?" "Yes!" And when help comes along, we can't afford to be selective about what type of help we want. We have to be willing to accept the help that God makes available. And He may have to send help from more than one source. With all of our well-intentioned eagerness, our help was not enough to solve the problem. The collective help brought about change. Even still, the woman in distress had to ultimately get the problem fixed. When God offers help, we still have to make an effort and then get what's wrong fixed, repaired, corrected. His help and our effort bring about the necessary change.

Tetanus Shots

Hear instruction, and be wise, and refuse it not. Proverbs 8:33

It is a harsh truth that the very thing used to help us sometimes hurts. At my annual physical, which involved painful procedures I don't dare even whisper, the nurse discovered that it had been 9 years since my last Tetanus shot. This shot, recommended every 10 years, is used to prevent those who sustain deep cuts or puncture wounds, which get infected, from developing the serious effects of Tetanus. The primary symptom of this condition is prolonged contraction of muscles, including lockjaw. It can also affect the heart, as it too is a muscle. "Well, you're almost at ten years, so why don't we just go ahead and give you the shot today?" she asked, cheerfully, while taking my blood pressure. Her suggestion did not evoke cheer in me. In fact, my blood pressure proved to be slightly higher than usual . . . very likely attributable to my hatred of needles and the impending shot. The chipper nurse returned with a vial and syringe and informed me that the drug had now been advanced and combined with the Pertussis vaccine to protect you against Tetanus and the Whooping Cough. The new shot, while more effective, also causes a bit more . . . well, pain. "This is going to hurt in the next couple days . . . slight stick." And with that, my bubbly nurse poked the needle into my left shoulder. I took it like a man, commenting, "I've had a baby . . . I can take anything." Two days later I was whining like a baby. My upper arm was hot to the touch and even sorer than it was hot. A large knot formed under the skin and I found myself rubbing it to try to ease the pain. The dull ache claimed my attention sporadically throughout the 7 or so days of discomfort. So, the shot hurt and the after effects were less than pleasant. But, were I to risk it, how much more disquieting would Tetanus or the

Whooping Cough proved to have been? I needed to take the pain in order to inoculate myself against future pain and suffering. And there are times when those who love us give us something tantamount to a Tetanus shot. The help they administer hurts, like painful advice or the truth. It's a shot in the arm. And it may smart for a few days, but if it protects us from prolonged constriction of our senses or spares us the painful embarrassment of coughing up words we only wish we could choke back down, then amen. I'm glad I took the shot. And as much as I love to talk, the thought of lockjaw scares me more than needles. So for the friends and loved ones who administer their brand of Tetanus shots, I say, "thank you, Jesus." The prophet Nathan gave King David a spiritual Tetanus shot when he told him the truth about his disgusting greed in taking Bathsheba and then getting her husband killed in order to hide his sin. *(2 Samuel 1-24)* The shot did nothing to undo what he had already done in the past, nor did it eliminate the consequences of his actions, but I'd like to think it helped to protect him against some other instances of future hurt. Shots can do that. Now might be a good time for you to roll up your sleeve and . . .

The 2 Dids

The law of the Lord is perfect, converting the soul: the testimony of the Lord is sure, making wise the simple. The statutes of the Lord are right, rejoicing the heart: the commandment of the Lord is pure, enlightening the eyes. The fear of the Lord is clean, enduring forever: the judgments of the Lord are true and righteous altogether. Psalm 19:7-9

My dad is a pillar of wisdom. He has led a life rich with experience and is always eager to share these jewels with us. While he is a very knowledgeable man, his knowledge is often communicated in ways that are rather comical. If you aren't careful, the depth of his lessons can be lost in the humor. But he almost always reinforces the instruction with reminders or repeats. Over the years this reinforcement has become something we, his adoring children, eagerly anticipate because we know it will likely be colorful and amusing, but, more than that, useful in a very practical way. He has our best interest at heart. And he wants us to learn simply so that we can follow the instructions and benefit. For example, one summer my dad came to Seattle to visit my daughter and me. Our home had an attached garage with an entry into the living room. One night after dinner, we were so enjoying our visit that we wore ourselves out laughing and listening to his stories. Eventually we all retired for the night. The next morning, we awoke to find that I had somehow left the garage door open and had also left the door into the house unlocked. The house was totally unsecured. When my dad and I realized this, we were, of course, shocked and couldn't help but rehearse all of the potential tragedies that could have occurred as a result of leaving the house open all night as we slept. All ended with, "we could all be dead" this morning. So my dad admonished me to always double check both doors before Brookie and I went to bed. He was naturally concerned about whether I would be able to follow these instructions once he had returned to Connecticut. So after telling me at least ten times, with the mandatory, "someone could come in here and . . ." along with the, "I want to make sure nothing happens to you and Brookie," warning statements, he decided to give me one of his patent forms of reinforcement, of the clever and comical sort. I found it when I came home from work one afternoon. Taped to the interior of the entry door from the garage was a hand-written note, penned by my father, on a wrinkled piece of paper and affixed with brown packaging tape. It read:

The Two Dids

1. *Did you close the garage door?*
2. *Did you lock this door?*

   I could not help but chuckle, and that was the reaction of every visitor who came into our home and inquired about the note. His warning reminder, though somewhat comical, was effective. So much so that we never made the mistake of leaving those two doors open again. Furthermore, when we moved to our next home with an attached garage, we taped that very note to the interior door. It's there now, reminding me not only to make sure that the house is secure, but that my father loves me and wants my daughter, my brother and me to be safe. The laws established by my Heavenly Father are designed with the same thing in mind. They may not be comical, but they lovingly reinforce His desire that we be safe. Instead of looking at them as the 10 Don'ts, lets view them as the 10 Dids. Did you follow each to make sure that nothing happens to you? *Psalm 19:10 More to be desired are they than gold, yea, than much fine gold: sweeter also than honey and the honeycomb.*

Through

Yea, though I walk through the valley of the shadow of death, I will fear no evil: for thou art with me; thy rod and thy staff they comfort me. Psalm 23:4

The 23rd Psalm is a very popular one. Most can recite it from memory. I'm sure part of what makes it so popular and widely used is that it gives assurances that things will eventually be all right. It starts beautifully with the promise that we won't have to want for anything, and it ends with the promise that our enemies will get an "in your face" demonstration on our behalf and then we'll dwell with the Lord forever. But right in the middle there's this common word that says quite a bit. It's the word, "through." And sometimes we get hung up on that word. I want to encourage you about the nature of "through." I love that word, especially in the way it's used in the text above. It's intriguing to me because, in this sense, the word denotes forward motion. Yet, usually when we get to this part of the passage, we often see dark clouds forming and begin to hear the cold, eerie winds of doom blowing, chilling our very souls. We clutch our cloak and hunch our shoulders and drearily move toward the distant horizon where our hope and help will be realized. And sometimes it seems to be far off in the distance . . . so far, in fact, that we may even doubt its existence. Then there's that word I like, "through" . . . and through suggests that the place where we are in this valley of the shadow of darkness has an end point. Through is not permanent. It's the period between God providing: "The Lord is my Shepherd, I shall not want" . . . and God bringing us to the victorious end He has promised: "Surely goodness and mercy shall follow me all the days of my life and I shall dwell in the house of the Lord, forever." The question remains, how do you get through, 'through'? It's all a matter of perception. Through is not a destination; it is a route. So I take this series of roads, streets and highways to get to work each day. My office building is my final destination. I don't get to I-5, pull over and just sit there. I-5 isn't the place I'm ultimately trying to reach. It's just on the way. If I keep moving, I get to my office. I have to go through traffic to get there, and sometimes the traffic jam is annoying and nerve wracking, but I keep inching along and trust that if I keep moving I'll reach the desired destination . . . where I can dwell, and receive my reward—a paycheck. But we let the traffic jams and annoyances and even the pain and the loneliness . . . sometimes the depression and the heartache of the valley of the shadow of death make us feel trapped. Then we begin to make mistakes that keep us in 'through'. We even execute wrong turns that slow down the process of getting through. Through isn't intended to be a permanent location. So how do we endure through and get through? I want to give you a vital instruction (that hopefully I'll be able to follow myself), which I hope will get you through. Here it is . . . Keep moving! That's it. You thought it was going to be some deep, philosophical thing. Nope. Just keep moving. There are benefits to going through. If you can get through, you will be better for having gone through. Here's why . . . *Hebrews 12:11: Now no chastening for the present seemeth to be joyous, but grievous: nevertheless afterward it yieldeth the peaceable fruit of righteousness unto them which are exercised thereby.* Simply put, the beating that we feel like we are taking on our way through 'through' may not be a pleasant experience, but it will prove to be a fruitful one. It gets us steps closer to the righteousness we desire, as well as the goodness and mercy that will follow. Keep moving.

Uppy

. . . He shall gather the lambs with his arm, and carry them in his bosom . . . . Isaiah 40:11

Toddlers love to be picked up. They spend much of their first months of development being held. When they begin to feel twinges of independence, they suddenly want to get down. They wiggle out of the laps of those holding them. They slide feet first down from beds and chairs where they've been placed. They even plot and plan great escapes from their cribs, sometimes risking life and limb to get out. I've heard stories of how parents peeked through bedroom doors to see how their baby was actually getting out of his crib. The discovery was frightening as they watched the child stack toys in the corner of the crib in order to climb out, then, swinging his little body over the railing, he would hang there for a second or two before doing a free fall to the floor. Then, he would crawl to where the rest of the family could be found. Toddlers are driven by the desire to walk. Yet, even with the desire for independence, they often tug at the pants of those to whom they must look up. And then, reaching up, utter the childish request, "Uppy!" Having spent all that time trying to get down, they still want to be picked up every now and then. And the desire to be picked up sometimes gets so strong that they begin to cry or even threaten to throw a tantrum in order to be picked up. More than requesting, they are insisting on being picked up. It's urgent. In this picture is revealed just how childlike we can be. We crave independence and work hard to stand on our own two feet. But every now and then, we need to be lifted. This is especially true when we grow weary or when everything and everyone around us seems to tower above us. Although I'm all grown up, at least somewhat, and self-reliant in so many aspects of my life, I'm still my Father's child. And one of the most endearing characteristics of our relationship is the tender way in which He desires to embrace and care for me. When the "big girl" world gets to be a bit much, emotionally I see myself, arms reaching toward the sky as I cry out, "Uppy!" I want the Father to pick me up. Being carried in His safe arms, I gain a different perspective on things around me. Eventually, I'll be ready to get down and walk on my own again, but for now, I'm comfortable with being carried by the One with arms strong enough to hold me. I'm uplifted. I'm humble enough to let Him pick me up and carry me. I'm grateful that I have a Father who is willing to lift me up. *Humble yourselves in the sight of the Lord and He will lift you up. (James 4:10)* Enjoy the lift.

Do You See What I See?

. . . Eyes have they, but they see not . . . Psalm 115:5

My father is a puzzle buff. He scours the Sunday paper looking for crossword puzzles, word-finds and other games that will capture his attention and fill a couple hours of his day. He's retired. But even before he retired from work as a machine operator, I remember seeing him sitting at the dining room table working his puzzles. He's actually pretty good at them, in fact. One such game, I guess you could call it, that he has conquered is the stereogram. A stereogram is an optical illusion, which contains a hidden 3 dimensional image. It requires parallel viewing to see the hidden image. Parallel viewing is the act of looking through a solid object, as if you are looking through a window. When you train your eyes upon a stereogram and look at it in a certain way, a 3-D image appears. It's sort of a picture within a picture. My father would often challenge me to look for the hidden picture. He would attempt to give me instructions on how to adjust my eyes so that I could get a glimpse of what he saw. I would cross my eyes and blur my vision in a usually fruitless attempt to see this hidden image. The only things that seemed to materialize for me were a headache and frustration. My father would even tell me what to look for so that if I did catch a faint glimpse of the hidden image, I could then focus on it. Still, seldom did I see anything other than lines, colorful patterns and, well, nothing. To do parallel viewing, you must aim your eyes through an image and into the distance. For me, the harder I tried to see this seemingly invisible object, the more frustrated I became and less likely I was to see anything. Meanwhile, my father, an experienced stereogram viewer, could see each hidden image and boasted of his ability. It must have been a skill he acquired during his difficult years of oppression growing up in the Deep South, but looking to a better life, which wasn't immediately visible. Then one day he told me to stop trying so hard and just look. Suddenly the image appeared. I was ecstatic, feeling as though I had just solved a problem in quantum physics. When I stopped looking so hard and let go of my frustrations, the image was right before my eyes. My father had taught me to see what was not clearly visible although it was right in front of me. Throughout his Christian walk, he has attempted to teach me that type of lesson in faith. And Our Heavenly Father is trying to do the same for us. He is trying to show us the hidden treasures of things to come. He wants us to train our eyes so that we can bring into focus what the patterns of life and perplexities tend to hide from us. To see the hidden image will require parallel vision. The ability to see what is all around us, in the here and now, but also see the glory of heaven in the distance. This means we will have to look right through our current circumstances, as if through a window. Right now we see through a glass, darkly (1 Corinthians 13:12). Once our eyes are trained, we will see that the image is not so hidden. It's there for all to see. John 14:1-4 tells us just what the picture is. It's our Father's house with many rooms that is being prepared for us as I yet type. Can't you see it?

Does it Really Work?

And all things, whatsoever ye shall ask in prayer, believing, ye shall receive. Matthew 21:22

It was prayer request time in the classroom at the little Christian school. One first grade student was asked if he had a prayer request and his response was quite unexpected. "No," he said, adding, "It doesn't work." The teacher asked why he thought such a thing. "Because my eyes were "howarting and I pwayed and they are still howarting." He looked up at her with those big, round, blue, hurting eyes, and she searched desperately for the right answer to give this 6 year old. She needed an answer that he could understand and that would restore his juvenile faith in prayer. "Well, Josh, God doesn't always answer our prayers immediately. That doesn't mean that prayer doesn't work. It just means that God is planning to answer our prayer in His own way and in His time." She added that it's our job to keep praying and waiting for our answer. When the account was shared with me, I couldn't help hoping that God would, with expedience, stop that little lad's eyes from hurting so that he could believe in prayer again. Wouldn't it be nice if God answered all of our prayers with immediacy so that we could see the successful results of prayer and trust the One answering the prayer all the more? Were this how prayer worked, would it really increase our faith, though? Probably not. What it would likely do is increase our level of expectation and make us less grateful for answered prayer. God is not in the business of manning the request line and giving us made to order answers. His slogan isn't "Have it your way." That would be Burger King. He is King of Kings. And as such, He knows what we need and when it's best to give it to us. Many times our failure to get our desired answer is based on our lack of belief. Other times God, having assessed our motives as less than healthy, elects not to grant the request. And still there are times when His will for us differs than our will for ourselves. If we have asked that His will be done, in our request, we have to be prepared to accept the fact that His will may not render the answer we desire. I don't know why Josh's eyes continued to hurt after he had asked God to take away the pain. I don't know when and how God will answer that little boy's request. But I do know that prayer works even when the answer doesn't match the request. I know because I have had many a prayer answered in ways only God could. God hears us and is not ignoring us. He is working on our behalf even before we ask. So don't stop praying. It works. And sometimes we just need eyeglasses to see how well it works.

A World Rocking Walk to Remember...

. . . when my heart is overwhelmed, I go to the rock that is higher than I. Psalm 61

First, let me say that I didn't want to do it. Walking was NOT on my 'woe is me' schedule of activities for this obnoxiously sunny Sunday. When you are feeling sorry for yourself, sunshine somewhat ruins the effect. Anyway, following the advice of some really dear friends who love me and called me to encourage me (including my girl Lisa who made me laugh with her theories on "punklivity" and methods of combating it), I decided to go for the prescribed power-walk. Sometimes when you are feeling low, even walking is a major feat. I grabbed my iPod, put on my headset, stretched and took to the walking trail along the greenbelt—so named with beautiful reason—which extends for miles near my home. Setting my iTunes to an upbeat, contemporary rock song on repeat, I walked, jogged, and skipped, stopping periodically to dance, for about 4 miles. During that hour, a positive change began to take place in me. I'm not sure if it was the endorphins that kicked in, the vitamin D from the needed sunshine, the thumping song that served as the soundtrack for my motivational walk or the prayers that friends were sending up for me as I performed this unplanned exercise. As I walked, I became aware of some things that my sleepy, oxygen deprived brain might never have gained the benefit of recognizing had I stayed in bed watching Lifetime movies and eating carbohydrates like I wanted to, had I not been bullied out of bed. My brain processed some cool things. There are countless shades of green. Shadows can be as beautiful as the objects they imitate. All weeds aren't ugly. New Balance makes really good running shoes. More than that, I took notice of some really powerful life object lessons. As I walked the winding,

154

hilly path, I realized that in several areas, those walking or riding on the trail had veered off course and created shortcuts in an effort to avoid the wide bends and reduce the mileage of the established, paved trail. The shortcut paths were rocky and bumpy. I pondered whether those who took that path were wise or foolish, but then decided that I had no right to judge. After all, the two paths ultimately led to the same end. Getting to the end and accomplishing the journey was all that mattered in that instance. I saw signs alerting walkers to the fact that there were many species of birds on the path and suggesting that the reader attempt to identify them. All I saw were two yellow birds, a few soul chickens aka crows, and a hawk. I was interested to see that they were all flying together. Another object lesson about camaraderie and the equal opportunity sky. I experienced brief moments of irritation from having to look at litter and debris from idiotic and inconsiderate people who clearly didn't appreciate the loveliness of nature . . . and rude reminders that not every dog walker obeys the pooper-scooper ordinance. But my mild aggravation melted away each time my eyes took in the splendor of the residual spring flowers, which, in defiance of the hot summer sun, refused to wilt and showed off their true colors. Four miles later, I decided to be that daisy. My friends could now be uninvited to join me at my pity party. There was no need to RSVP. The party was cancelled. Oh, I still planned to have my cake (courtesy of that same friend), but I wouldn't be crying in my ice cream . . . . Not on that particular day anyway. And to the possibly lonely and sad person reading this reading this, we rock! It took a walk to help me realize that. Okay, for the humorless religious zealot bothered by the fact that I dared to use a song other than a hymn to make my spiritual illustration, insert Rock of Ages.

*Punklivity = One's tendency to act like a punk.

Can't Live Without It

And she said, The Philistines be upon thee, Samson. And he awoke out of his sleep, and said, I will go out as at other times before, and shake myself. And he wist not that the LORD was departed from him. Judges 16:20

I don't want to tell you why you need the anointing of God. I'd rather tell you why you don't want to live without it. There are two scenarios of major interest to me in the Word, both detailing the significance of being the anointed of God. They vividly describe the blessing of being given this anointing . . . but they also painfully describe the tragedy of having the anointing taken away. I am referring to Eli and his rotten sons; and Samson and his rotten attitude. They both had been given something that cannot be easily attained. We live in an age when human beings are able to obtain and acquire just about anything. We pride ourselves on the luxuries, conveniences, and possessions to which we are able to lay sometimes immediate claim. Given the time, money, and opportunity we can achieve and obtain nearly anything we want, if we want it badly enough. We live in country where anything is possible and nearly everything is accessible. Yet, a great deal of what we desperately seek isn't really necessary. In fact we can live without much of what we want. But there are some things of immeasurable value, which we cannot simply run out and get. One such thing is vital, whether or not we are aware of it. And despite the fact that many of us do not seek it, the truth is we can't live without it. I am talking about the presence of God . . . the anointing of God. Desperately needed . . . yet appreciated less than some of our possessions. Whether or not we recognize it, we really don't want to live WITHOUT the anointing. It is said, "You don't miss the water till the well runs dry." Sometimes you don't even miss it then, because you aren't conscious of the loss.

The first colorful story begins in I Samuel, Chapter 3. Eli was given the task of training up a prophet. Hannah, after having prayed so hard for a son that she appeared drunk, was given a child at long last. Honoring the promise she made to God to give this child to the service of the Lord, she brings Samuel to Eli. Eli recognizes this child has the anointing of God because God has spoken to the young lad. Now, the sons of Eli, Hophni and Phinehas, presided over the temple. One would have thought that they, as priests and leaders, would have had the anointing of God as well. One would have thought that by virtue of their position they would have been operating under the unction of the Spirit of God. Yet, their actions . . . the raping and pillaging of the church and parishioners, were evidence that the Spirit of God was not with them. They had the priestly garb, but it was just for show. In fact, the anointing that was upon Israel was taken away because of their foolishness. They even lost the Ark of the Covenant. Here is where the downfall begins. In the 4th chapter, the Israelites are losing in battle, pitifully. They send for the Ark of the Covenant as if it contains magic. Their anointing is gone, but they feel if they can get the magic ark, they can rub it, say some mumbo-jumbo and, presto, they can win again. So the ark is brought to them and they cheer. Their shout is so loud, it shakes the ground. The Philistines hear the shout and panic. They inquire what the noise is about and they are told the ark has been brought. They recall what happened to Pharaoh's army and they don't want to go up against these people who have the ark. You see the Israelites shouted . . . they made a whole lot of noise . . . but they had no anointing! Now they go to battle and are defeated by the Philistines. The rest of the story is increasingly tragic. A messenger runs to tell 98-year-old Eli that his sons have been slain in battle and the ark lost and he falls over backwards in his chair, breaks his neck, and dies. Then his daughter-in-law, Phinehas's wife, upon hearing the bad news goes into labor and dies in childbirth, but not before naming her son Ichabod—meaning "Israel's glory is gone." Not only was the ark gone, the sons of Eli gone, and the priest himself, but the anointing was gone. Can't live without it.

Samson suffered a similar fate. People love to blame Delilah. Now I'll grant you she was a satanic beauty, but Samson's pride and lust for power, popularity, and celebrity—co-mingled with disobedience, are what led to his demise. The anointing of God was upon Samson. But he used it like a circus act or a sideshow. Like many of us, he got caught up in the external gifts of the anointing. The trappings, if you will. Pride and the anointing cannot co-exist. King Saul is another prime example.

Well, you've just read a whole lot of bad news, but here's the good part. God wants each of us to dwell within His presence and He desires to anoint us with His Spirit so that we can have power to live right, power to honor Him, power to minister, power to serve, power to obey. Maybe some of us once had the anointing and have somehow lost it . . . some of us may not even know that the Spirit has departed from us . . . walking dead men and women. But in this hour, in this moment we can reclaim or get back what we've lost. Some of us may feel like we are in bondage in our lives, shackled to foolishness. The Word of God tells us that the anointing destroys the yoke. You want to be set free . . . it's in His anointing. And maybe there are others still who are eagerly seeking a fresh anointing, rededicating their lives to the One who gave life. God is faithful and He will give it back. Eyes, gouged out, hair cut, dignity gone, Samson now realized through his blindness what he couldn't see when he had sight. He sees the need for the presence of God. He sees the need for the anointing of God. He prays a simple prayer and asks a child to lead him to the pillars that are holding up the weight of what pulled him down. He places his hands on the beams and pushes with all His might. In this moment the power of God, the presence of God, the anointing of God returns and, though it costs him his life, he gets back what he couldn't live without. I don't know where you are in your spiritual experience or in your life, but I do know that you can't live without the power and the anointing of God. You might exist but you won't live without it. And as an act of faith, I want to encourage you, yes you, to seek out a God-fearing, sincere elder; maybe one at your church or a trusted friend. Ask them to anoint you with oil, in the Name of Jesus, connecting your faith with God's power. There is no power in the oil, but there is power in our faith. This ceremonious act is symbolic . . . yet if you will dare to seek it in faith and ask for the anointing of God in your life as this oil is applied, you can have the assurance that the blood also has been applied. We need the anointing . . . can't live without it. We put all kinds of stock in oil as fuel, let's recognize the value of the anointing oil to provide power for our journey.

Just Stand Up

Wherefore take unto you the whole armor of God, that ye may be able to withstand in the evil day, and having done all, to stand.
Ephesians 6:13

I was drowning. Somehow the water had gotten over my head and a wonderful afternoon of water play at the beach had now turned deadly for me, or so I thought. Thrashing in the water, my whole 9 or 10 years of life now flashing before my waterlogged eyes, I cried out for help. I could see my brother, Bobby, standing near the shore, seemingly ignoring my desperate call to rescue me. If I survived this, I would get him back for sure. Every penny in my piggy bank would be spent on itching powder . . . I'd short sheet his bed or eat the entire stash of candy in his dresser drawer . . . but now for the matter of drowning. Just how I wound up in the deep water was beyond me. I must have gone out further than I realized, but my brother could save me, if only he would. Instead, there he stood watching me flounder and ultimately succumb to the ravaging waters of the deep. Amid the screaming and the crashing sounds of the water about my head, I heard him saying something. I could barely make out his words, "Up!" He yelled to me. What?! What was he saying, and why was he trying to carry on a conversation with me while I was in a frantic water fight for my life? Again, "J . . . St . . . Up!" "Stup?" . . . Huh? What did that mean? I'm drowning and he's giving me some code language. Tiring at this point and seeing the credits of my life rolling, I strained to hear what he was yelling from the safety of the shore. Finally! I heard him. "Stand up! Just stand up!" And so I did. I stopped my wild flailing and . . . stood up. When I did, the water was barely up to my chest. Gasping for breath and exhausted, I walked out of the water and to the shore where my brother, now laughing, stood waiting to greet me. From the shore he could see that the water wasn't all that deep. He knew that all I had to do was stand up and I'd be fine. Sure, he could have walked out into the water and pulled me up by one arm, but aside from enjoying watching his pain in the neck, kid sister splashing foolishly, he wanted to see me exercise common sense and help myself. He knew if I just stood up, I'd be fine. He was right.

I'm not 10 anymore, haven't been for over 30 years, but I've found myself drowning a few times since. Clearly in over my head in a situation, I'm floundering. Circumstances in my life making me feel as though I'm about to succumb, I tire. Then I hear my brother's words. "Just stand up." When I've listened and taken the prescribed action, I've been able to walk out of the situation—exhausted, but safe. When I haven't immediately followed the simple instructions, I've continued sinking and drowning nearly to the point of spiritual death. I don't know, maybe I'm not alone. Are you in over your head? Perhaps you've gone further than you realized and now you're in a situation that you feel you'll never get out of alive. A relationship, vice, or self-destructive occupation that has you going down for the third time. May I offer you the same suggestion offered to me by my then teenage brother? Try to just stand up. The situation may not be as deep as you think it is. I want to encourage you to just stand up. You see, our brother, Jesus, is on the shore poised to rescue us, yet He wants us to make an effort to stand. He'll pull us out when we reach for Him, but He has given us the power to stand. Having put on the life-vest of righteousness, and done everything we can do, we merely need to stand.

Theory of Relativity

Rejoice with them that do rejoice, and weep with them that weep.
Romans 12:15

We as human beings tend to think that our problems are worse than those of others. My aging father often makes us laugh with his sometimes shocking observations and statements. In response to my complaint of illness once, he responded, "You weren't as sick as I was." The response made me forget that I was sick and sparked muffled laughter on my part. He then went on to list all of his maladies in great detail, which prompted more stifled laughter. "I had body aches and pains, chills and fevers, nose running like a faucet . . . and my feets were cold." By then I was nearly doubled over in restrained laughter. Not that I doubted the validity of his sickness nor disputed the severity of it in comparison to my own, but the fact that he would first of all dismiss my symptoms and then recite his own was comical to me in such a cute way. The truth of the matter is that we often feel that we are worse off than others . . . until we learn of someone's situation that is clearly far more serious than our own. Even then, we still feel as though we are suffering because pain is relative. You may have lost both mother and father to death, but the loss of my loved one hurls me into just as deep a pit of sorrow. Certainly there are those who have endured traumatic circumstances that far surpass that of common disappointment. But for the one experiencing the disappointment, the trauma is real. Knowing this, we are drawn to the passage of scripture that reads, bear one another's burdens. We are to weep with those who weep and mourn with those who mourn. Why? Because each of us has his or her own cross to bear, and the pain of the experience is relative. Never discount the suffering of another, because you do not know all of the ramifications of that person's distress. Instead, pray for them and offer them not only sympathy but also empathy. No matter how you view their situation, remember your own and how you have desired encouragement. This makes us more prone to offer what we know we have needed. Christ looked into the hearts of those to whom He ministered. He saw their pain and hurt and offered relief. He didn't qualify or quantify their suffering, saying, "Well, this man is crippled in only one leg so I won't bother healing him. He can make it with a cane." He simply ministered to the sick, realizing their pain was relative. This is because He felt their pain and responded to it. As Christians, it is our duty, likewise, to minister to those who suffer in one way or another. Through prayer, exhortation or whatever means we have available to us. Comfort ye my people. Support the weak.

Simply Stop

What shall we say then? Shall we continue in sin, that grace may abound? God Forbid. Romans 6:1-2

There was an official letter on the kitchen counter from the City of Seattle. It was addressed to me. I would soon find that it wasn't because I was important. My brother had already opened it out of curiosity, and before I could settle into the idea that this was some letter of commendation or recognition from the Mayor praising me for community activism or civic heroism, he announced that it was a traffic ticket. There would be no ticker-tape parade in my honor. But I would have my fifteen minutes of fame. Apparently, I had been caught by the city's new traffic cameras, running a red light. There it was, in bold, vivid color . . . photographic evidence of my traffic violation. There were actually 3 photographs, one of which was a zoom shot of my license plate. There was no denying it or getting around it. I was caught. I remembered the night the offense took place. I was speeding along Rainier Ave., on my way to pick up my daughter from the home of friends. I was tired, it was getting late, and I had grown annoyed with the other "slow poke" drivers on the road. I had just passed one such indecisive motorist and suddenly the light turned yellow, then red. I figured I was moving too fast to safely stop so I went ahead and raced through the clear intersection, running the not amber, not soft orange, but bright RED light. Just then there was a flashing light, which I was sure was a police car, but when no patrol car pursued me, I thought I had escaped the punitive action I was due. What I didn't realize is that the flashing light was that of the camera which had recorded my flagrant disregard for the traffic laws. Now 3 weeks later, my punishment had come to my home address in an official capacity. All I could do was laugh at myself. While my brother and my friend, Sue, examined the photographs and, like criminal attorneys, mulled over my possible legal recourse and how I might find a loophole through which to avoid paying this fine, I promptly retrieved my debit card from my purse and went on the Internet to pay the price for my misdeed. I couldn't even in good conscience look for a way out. I knew that I was guilty . . . and so did Sue, because she was in the car with me at the time of my high-speed disobedience. She might easily have been considered an accomplice even though she wasn't behind the wheel. You know what they say about guilt by association. But I was the one driving and I was the one who failed to stop. I had just learned a costly lesson, to the tune of $101.00. Well, guess what? If we fail to obey God's laws and make the decision to continue speeding ahead in error without stopping, our violations will be caught on tape and there will be a price to pay . . . a heavy price. I felt I had gone too far to stop so I decided to continue through the red light. We sometimes feel the same way in our sinful actions. We think we've gone so far we may as well continue on. It's too late to stop now, we tell ourselves. But nothing could be further from the truth. The devil wants us to keep going and even accelerate down the path of madness, ignoring the flashing red lights. God wants us to know that no matter how far we've gone, it's not too late to stop. Put on the brakes! You're at the intersection of right and wrong. Simply stop! That's all . . . stop.

Rainbow Promises

I have placed my rainbow in the clouds. It is the sign of my covenant with you and with all the earth. Genesis 9:13 NLT

It had been an especially discouraging and stressful day. I was working in a mental health program that was certainly putting my own to the test. As I dealt with a caseload of 8 individuals who were suffering from various forms and degrees of psychosis, I must admit the medication began to look good to me. On this particular day it seems there had been one crisis after another and I felt as if I were taking on some of the symptoms exhibited by my clients. When the workday finally ended, I was now facing the hour-long commute home, in the pouring rain. As I made my way up the on ramp to the highway I was sentenced to travel, the rain suddenly stopped and rays of sun forced their way through the clouds, opening up a patch of blue in the sky. I sighed with relief. Then as I rounded the curve, a different area of sky now came into view and, to my utter delight, there was the most brilliant rainbow I had ever seen in my life. It was so vibrant that travelers had stopped along the highway and gotten out of their vehicles to get a better view of this spectacle. I drove along slowly in stunned silence, mesmerized by its beauty. Tears came to my eyes. I thanked God for this colorful reminder that He cared. He had seen each trial of the day that threatened to sink me. He knew by the end of the day that I had experienced my own version of 40 days and 40 nights of rain and psychosis. And I'm sure He was thinking about all the others who had been through their own agonies on that day and needed a rainbow to restore their sense of hope. I was grateful. "Thank you, God," I whispered. He had allowed the rain to give way to sunshine, making a rainbow possible. I watched the sky until the rainbow was no longer visible, but even after I could no longer see it; the colorful image was burned into my mind's eye. The drive home seemed shorter and the cares of the day less overwhelming. Thanks be to God, He had given us a sign that, yes, He's there. That's the kind of loving God we serve. He reminds us of the covenant or promise He's made. He honors his promises and never leaves us comfortless. That rainbow was like a sedative for me. It calmed my emotional meltdown, not through hypnosis or mind-control. But through the reassurance that God is still in control and can, at His will, stop the rain, cause the sun to shine in our lives, and bring color to our grey and darkened experience. There will be times in our lives when we feel inconsolable. In such times reflect on the rainbow promise and be comforted. I once heard a saying that "above the clouds, the sun is always shining." If ever you have flown on an airplane during a rainstorm, you know this to be true. As the plane ascends above the rain clouds, and reaches a certain altitude, you're surprised to see how sunny it is above the clouds. When hysteria prevails, allow God to help you rise above it on the wings of His love and with the knowledge of His promises. *Peace I leave with you, my peace I give unto you: not as the world giveth, give I unto you. Let not your heart be troubled, neither let it be afraid. John 14:27KJV*

Training Wheels

Train up a child in the way he should go and when he is old he will not depart from it. Proverbs 22:6

Letting go can be a really difficult thing to do. Especially when it involves those we love. The kind side of human nature wants to nurture. But there comes a time when we have to release our grip, pray, and allow our older children or others to, well, ride. Allow me to explain. When my sister Marionette bought my daughter her first bike, my dad, the resident bike-riding teacher, took on Brookie as his new student. He thought it best to make sure the bike be equipped with training wheels. I watched as he placed her on the little pink bike with streamers on the handlebars, a basket, and a bell, and gave her a gentle push to get her going. "Pedal!" he told her, and that she did. With all the might her little legs could muster, she pedaled and headed, wobbling, down the road behind our home, my dad—her grandfather—running alongside her. After a few weeks of riding with the comforts of the training wheels, my dad decided it was time that he take them off and see what she could do on her own. Of course, being a nervous and overprotective mother—I'm finally able to admit it, I balked at the notion. As if he were going to now let her ride a motorcycle, I felt a bit panicky. "Let's just give her a couple more months," I suggested. But dad wasn't hearing that and, toolbox in hand, he marched right outside to upgrade my Brookie's bike from the baby model to the big girl model. Brooke, being a daredevil since birth, it seems, was thrilled that the training wheels were coming off and that she would get to ride freely. But she didn't quite realize the difference that training wheels can make. He placed her on the bike again, as if for the first time. He had taught her the art of steering the bike, stepping backwards on the

167

pedal to brake and all the other road safety rules. He reminded her of these again, as if reciting a checklist to a racecar driver, and with that began walking her down the road, holding the bike as she pedaled. She must have noticed the difference in not having her training wheels because she called out, "Hold me, Grandpa, hold me!" He assured her that he had her, but every now and then he would remove his hands from the bike and let her ride unsteadily along for a second or two on her own. I watched as if she were running with scissors. Finally, he let go completely and she was riding! She didn't even know his hands were no longer holding her up. My dad stopped running alongside her eventually and she pedaled to the end of the road, laughing that silly-girl laugh that has always been so contagious. There was a mixture of tears and laughter erupting from me. I won't tell you what happened at the end of the road because I don't want to wreck the glorious ending to the story. But it was nothing a small bandage couldn't fix. I lived through the experience and marveled at how she learned to ride without the training wheels so quickly. I am convinced that it wasn't so much the training wheels that gave her confidence to ride. They were barely even touching the ground in all actuality. But it was more likely the confidence of knowing that her grandfather was there to help her that taught her to ride on her own. And even when he let her go she knew he was still there. Sure, in subsequent weeks, she fell a few more times and scraped her knees. But she's still riding to this day. Now, she's even learning to drive a car. There comes a time when our children, nieces, nephews or other individuals whom we love and feel a certain sense of responsibility toward will need to be released from our loving grasp. Though it may make us nervous and pains us to think of them falling, we have to let go and let them ride. The counsel and loving instruction we have given them is the training wheels. We have taught them the rules of safety and advised them of how to stop. Now we have to let them ride, knowing that we are still there, and more importantly, that God is there. We learn to function as Christians with the use of training wheels; those things that keep us from toppling over. No one need be ashamed of the training wheels. They will help get us to the place where we can ride on our own. Then we'll still be able to ride safely, even when loving hands have let go.

Spiritual Flat Tires

Blessed are they which do hunger and thirst after righteousness: for they shall be filled. Matthew 5:6

If you've ever experienced the inconvenience of a flat tire, you know what a nuisance they can be. Especially if you don't know exactly how to change them, don't have help changing them or you lack the proper tools. Flat tires occur in different ways. Sometimes they are the result of running over a nail. Sometimes they are caused by a slow leak of which you weren't even aware. A flat tire is usually unexpected and happens at the most inopportune time, and they can prevent you from getting where you want to be. And a flat tire can deflate your whole countenance . . . just like that tire. There are times that we experience spiritual flat tires . . . and even blowouts. There we are, cruising down the highway of life, wind blowing through our hair . . . moving along at a steady clip when all of a sudden we begin to feel the bumping that indicates there's something wrong. Routinely living from day to day without the proper maintenance of serious prayer and study or even time with the Master Mechanic, we allow our tires, the things that carry us forward, to fall into disrepair. The treads are worn down and we don't have the correct amount of air in the tires. Perhaps we had a slow leak and by the time we make the discovery it's too late. Someone knows exactly what I'm talking about. We're spiritually flat and don't know exactly how to change it. As a result, we're getting nowhere. We suffer a worse fate when an actual blowout occurs because that can cause us to lose control. And if you continue to drive on a flat or blown-out tire for too long, you run the risk of ruining the wheel. I was talking with a co-worker and friend the other day, and she was telling me how her son had experienced a blow-out while driving her car that week and by the time he drove to a safe place to stop, the iron wheel itself had cracked. She was thankful that he was spared injury, but the wheel had to be repaired in addition to replacement of the tire. Some of us have attempted to continue driving on our spiritual flat, unaware that this may make matters worse. We've ignored the thudding and tried to pretend that everything was okay. But in truth, we need maintenance. A flat tire symbolizes emptiness, deflated hopes and dreams, perhaps even the depletion of faith, and an inability to move forward. A flat tire can't be filled with money or success. It doesn't need to be filled with expensive possessions or luxuries. It simply needs air. Trying to fill it with anything else would be futile. We may not know how to change a flat tire, but God does. He can breathe life back into you and fill you. Then, He can place you back on the road to progress with new wheels. Why am I speaking in parables? Well, besides the fact that it worked for Jesus, there are times when life can best be described by analogical experiences. And just as there are ways to solve life's everyday problems, so too are there ways to solve those of a spiritual nature. Allow God to maintain you and keep you in good condition. Your relationship with Him is where the rubber meets the road. At the first sign of a loss of air pressure, stop and take steps to be refilled. Spending time with a spiritually strong and trustworthy friend can sometimes re-inflate us. Join a Bible study or prayer group. The best method of spiritual repair is by simply seeking God. I will look to the hills from whence cometh my help . . . my help cometh from the Lord. (Psalm 121:1-2)

You'll Live

. . . But though our outward man perish, yet the inward man is renewed day by day. [17] For our light affliction, which is but for a moment, worketh for us a far more exceeding and eternal weight of glory; [18] While we look not at the things which are seen, but at the things which are not seen: for the things which are seen are temporal; but the things which are not seen are eternal. 2 Corinthians 4:16-18

There are those of us who face some crisis every day of our lives. Or so it seems. What may be viewed as a small or minor inconvenience to some is a catastrophic occurrence of gargantuan proportions to us. If we get a headache, it must be a tumor. A stomachache is most likely an ulcer. The slightest touch of heartburn is undoubtedly a heart attack and fatigue is, unfortunately, cancer. Alright, this may sound a bit extreme, but some of us tend to make our situations bigger than they actually are and consequently intensify our own suffering. The problem is, when we finally face a real challenge we have no idea how to deal with it. All of the experience that we have gathered during our tragedy practice amounts to nothing. We are spiritual hypochondriacs and despite what we know, we fear there is no remedy for our situation. Wouldn't we do much better if we learned to place our problems in proper perspective as light afflictions that ready us for the glory to come? That's what our spiritual journey is designed to teach us. As we overcome in each situation, we are to draw from it courage that will help us through the next set of trials. Anticipating the worst and becoming faint of heart plays right into the plan of the enemy to fill our hearts with dread and rob us of our hope. I have a teenage daughter whom I affectionately refer to as my Drama Queen. It is definitely an earned title. She is convinced that every discomfort in her life is going to kill her. I assure her she'll live but my announcement is met with skepticism. If she doesn't get the right outfits for school the world will definitely stop revolving . . . abruptly. And a broken fingernail would throw her world off kilter were it not for the reality checks administered regularly by her mother. Our Heavenly Father often gives us similar reality checks to pull us off the ledge of hopelessness. But the next time we suffer a hurt or pain, we sometimes crawl back out onto the ledge. Faith should teach us to hope for the best, not fear the worst. Knowing that the power of God is greater than anything that comes our way should fill us with confidence, even when the worst is a very real threat. There may be disappointments in our lives . . . that's par for the Christian course. Jesus issued an advisory that in the world you'll have tribulation . . . but He has overcome them all. Don't allow disappointment to steal your hope. I did some checking and it turns out that disappointment is not on the list of most life-threatening illnesses. Put problems in perspective. God is bigger than them, and so is the glory to come. Look to Him to bring you through even the worst. Regardless of what happens on this earth, with complete trust in God, ultimately you'll live . . . eternally.

My Angel

Be not forgetful to entertain strangers, for thereby some have entertained angels unawares.

Hebrews 13:2

I do believe angels exist. I believe they have blessed me many times, unknowingly, and at least once very obviously. No, I didn't experience a mystical encounter with a glowing being, shrouded in an aura of light. No heavenly choirs sang. No celestial orchestra. But on this particular day, I needed supernatural intervention. And that's exactly what I received. It was a chilly, rainy, Connecticut morning. My two-year-old daughter, Brooke, in arms, I limped into the local medical center for treatment of a knee injury. She thought we were on an adventure, as would most children of that age. Mommy had a funny walk, and this was somewhat entertaining to her. She played in the waiting room. Once in the examination room, her play continued. She reached for, touched, pulled, and attempted to climb on everything assembled in the room, which, in her estimation, was put there solely for her amusement. "You have a sprain. You'll need to take it easy with that knee and wear a brace for a couple weeks," the doctor announced. How on earth was I going to take it easy with a toddler? I could barely contain the busy baby within the confines of this exam room. Handing me a slip of paper with my "no" marching orders, she bid me farewell, bending to salute my miniature demolition derby. Moments later, we emerged from the building, my leg in a brace. And Brooke's play continued, as she delighted in the fact that she was being allowed to walk to the car instead being carried by mommy. On the way to the parking lot, a woman caught my eye. I glanced down at her feet curiously, wondering why she was wearing white shoes in winter. They were not-so-expensive pumps. (I have a shoe fetish, okay? I notice these things.) We greeted each other with a nod and she smiled at my bubbly little girl and me. In that split second, my little one, enjoying her newfound freedom from mommy's arms, decided she'd make a break for it. I had no idea how fast tiny legs could carry a person. As she darted across the lawn of the clinic, I panicked. On any other day she would have been no match for me. However, there was that little matter of the leg brace . . . you know, the thing that had mommy walking funny? I shouted for her to stop and hobbled in her direction, but this only made the game she thought we were playing more exciting. Laughing, she heightened the pace. The gap between us widened and I realized the situation was becoming very serious. The child was not heeding my calls to stop, but continued running—straight for the road. Mothers always having to be a step ahead of their children, I traced the path to where she was headed. Fear gripped my soul. My precious baby was going to reach the busy road before *I* could reach *her*. I screamed, "Please, Brookie, stop!" I may as well have told her to run faster, because that's what she did. I then looked at the road to see what we were up against. To my utter horror, of course there was a huge truck swiftly approaching. Tractor-trailer vs. toddler. You know the odds. Forsaking doctor's orders and defying the restraint of this device on my leg, I tried running, but there was no way of reaching her in time. Now hysterical, I saw a flash of what would be a tragic end. Suddenly the woman in the white shoes reappeared. She ran past me with what seemed like the speed of . . . well, an angel. Arms outstretched, she reached for my Brooke, whisking her away from the road just before the truck whizzed by. She scooped up my baby and carried her to me. Brookie was still laughing, never even realizing the danger she had just narrowly escaped. I stood paralyzed in tearful shock. Consoling me, she carried my daughter to my car. My arms were too weak to even hold Brooke. Once I regained my strength she handed her to me. I kissed my precious baby. When I turned to thank this kind woman, she was gone. I cannot tell you what she looked like. I have no recollection of her eye or hair color. All I remember is the white pumps, worn in winter, which ran to the rescue of my runaway toddler. I am convinced that on that chilly, rainy, Connecticut morning, I met an angel. No, she wasn't a glowing being, shrouded in an aura of light. She was wearing white pumps . . . in winter.

Doubting and Doing

I can do all things through Christ, which strengthens me.
Philippians 4:13

"It takes more energy to doubt than to do." That's the statement I made to a friend in discussing my hesitance to pursue a certain venture. His ever so clever response was, "By the time you finish doubting, you could have done what you doubted you could do." We laughed, but it was true. Too many times we spend so much time talking ourselves out of whatever it is we feel called or led to do. Our failure to achieve is less due to inability than inactivity. The fear of failure is paralyzing and doubt is the numbing agent. We exhaust ourselves with the "what ifs" of pessimism. What if I try it and it doesn't work out? What if this isn't really what God has in mind for me? What if there's something else I should be doing instead? What if? What if? What if? But what if, indeed? What if we stop looking for excuses to prevent us from stepping out in faith? Then, we might actually see the dream materialize, the hope realized, and the plans that God has for us come to pass. Shift from doubting and begin doing. The latter is so much more productive. Remember the text says, "I can DO all things through Christ, which strengthens me." It doesn't say I can doubt all things, or fear all things or put off attempting all things or fail at achieving all things. We tend to put the emphasis on "all" but before we can even get to the "all" we have to actually "do" something about it. Doubt gets in the way of success only if we let it. I only know one person whose doubting made him famous . . . or should I say infamous? Thomas, one of the 12 disciples whose doubt earned him the nickname "Doubting Thomas". He was also known as Didymus. (Check out the first three letters of that name and talk about irony.) In John, chapter 20, Jesus appears to some of the disciples after his resurrection, but Thomas is not present. John 20:25 says, *"So the other disciples told him, 'We have seen the Lord!' But he [Thomas] said to them, 'Unless I see the nail marks in his hands and put my finger where the nails were, and put my hand into his side, I will not believe it.'"* About a week later Jesus shows up again, as if to say, "If I don't make a reappearance, some of these called and chosen are not going to do what they have been called and chosen to do." This time Doubting Didy is in school for the lesson. *"Though the doors were locked, Jesus came and stood among them and said, 'Peace be with you!' Then he said to Thomas, 'Put your finger here; see my hands. Reach out your hand and put it into my side. Stop doubting and believe.' Thomas said to him, 'My Lord and my God!' Then Jesus told him, 'Because you have seen me, you have believed; blessed are those who have not seen and yet have believed'"*(John 20:26-29). And that's on the syllabus for the class you're now in on how to get it done. Don't wait until you see before you believe that you can do what God has in mind for you to do. I'm tempted to put in a famous Nike slogan here, but you get the point. The doubting ends here and the doing begins. By the way, what you're reading right now is the result of my actually doing what for so long I doubted.

Dream On

And Joseph was the governor over the land, and he it was that sold to all the people of the land: and Joseph's brethren came, and bowed down themselves before him with their faces to the earth. Genesis 42:6

Joseph was known as a dreamer. His weren't just pipe dreams but he dared to dream big. So big, in fact, that in his dreams he saw his brothers, father, and mother all bowing down to him. This dream represented something grand that God had in store for him, but his brothers were neither fascinated nor fond of his fanciful ideas. The dreams drove them to throw him in a pit and sell him into slavery. How would those dreams ever come true under such dire circumstances? I've wondered the same. Certainly while Joseph was in the pit, he wondered if maybe his lofty night visions may have been induced by the cabbage he ate at midnight. The years he spent in captivity as a slave had to cause him to further doubt the validity of his dream. And then he finds himself in prison as a result of an evil woman's false accusation and now his dream seemed to be completely dead. What do you do when you feel that your dream has died? When your hopes and what you have believed in seem near impossible? When the dream doesn't measure up with the actual? Joseph's disappointment was further compounded by the fact that he had always enjoyed favor. He was the clear favorite of his father; hence his brothers resented him and ultimately took revenge on him. Even in captivity he, for a season, enjoyed the favor of Potiphar, captain of the king's guard. Then there was the incident with the unreturned advances of his boss's wife and the cloak he left behind as he fled her seduction, and that comfortable arrangement abruptly ended. But Joseph had also been living in the favor of God, which seemed to have dried up as he sat in prison. Still, what he clung to is something that we tend to overlook when our dreams appear to have evaporated into thin air. That is the fact that with favor comes responsibility and often discipline and discomfort. Whom the Lord loveth, he chastens. (Hebrews 12:6) God sometimes will chastise us and allow us to endure hard trials as He prepares us for the realization of our dreams. This is His way of making us fit to carry out the dreams that He has inspired in us, when they do come to fruition. Were the dream to be easily achieved and without test or trial, its significance would be diminished and the miracle of it lost. And faith required that Joseph should hold onto the dream no matter how unrealistic, unlikely, and unusual it may have seemed. Imagine what a stand-up comedian Joseph would have been had he told his fellow prisoners that he would one day hold the position of a ruler. And all the while, God allowed Joseph to go on accurately interpreting the dreams of others while his own went yet unfulfilled. Those who promised not to forget about him, forgot about him. He spent 3 years in prison trying to stay alive, and even gained favor on lock-down, but his dream was still just that . . . a dream. No doubt at times he felt as if God had forsaken him. But the dream wasn't dead. All it needed to be sparked into reality was patience. Not the kind of 15-minute patience required to wait your turn at the nail salon or in the grocery checkout line while someone is getting a price check. Not even the kind of patience needed to wait for the timer on the microwave to signal that dinner is done. But, true patience that only comes with time and trust in God's sovereign plan. 5 long chapters and 13 years later, Joseph's dream was finally fulfilled. His brothers bowed before him as he stood as governor. He was eventually reunited with his father and his precious brother Benjamin. His patience had blossomed into something very real and tangible . . . a dream come true. *(Romans 5:3-4 ". . . but we glory in tribulations also: knowing that tribulation worketh patience; And patience, experience; and experience, hope: And hope maketh not ashamed . . .")* As you wait for your dream, which may seem to have died, to be realized, let patience have her perfect work. (James 1:4) That may be the final part of the process that God is waiting to see you develop. If He has given you the dream, no matter how far fetched, wait for it. It's not dead . . . it's just sleeping until God awakens it. Dream on.

Fear Factor

Fear not: for I have redeemed thee, I have called thee by thy name; thou art mine. When thou passest through the waters, I will be with thee; and through the rivers, they shall not overflow thee: when thou walkest through the fire, thou shalt not be burned; neither shall the flame kindle upon thee. Isaiah 43:1-2

Fear is, I believe, at the root of many poor choices or actions that we make. I'm certain research would back up my theory. For example, some individuals who knowingly marry the wrong individual or lead promiscuous lives likely do so because they fear loneliness. The substance abuser fears what life is like without his self-prescribed anesthesia. People lie because they fear the consequences of telling the truth. Cheating, stealing and a list of other less than noble behaviors could probably be easily linked to some form of fear. Fear paralyzes and instigates. Fear stymies and prompts. And in each case, Satan hovers above the unsuspecting puppet, pulling the strings as puppet master. If we could come to grips with those fears, whatever they may be, and present them to God in a very real way, we could cut the strings and hasten in the direction of victory. But fear itself often prevents us from even getting to the root of our fear. We don't really want to uncover it because then we would have to face it. Several years ago, a television program was introduced called Fear Factor. While I never liked the program, I caught a glimpse of it a time or two while looking, in vain, for another program with at least some redeeming value. The theme of this program was for contestants to undertake dangerous, horrifying and often repulsive exercises as they compete for money. They were required to lie in a vat of snakes, spiders or rats. Some were known to eat all manner of vile, otherwise inedible creatures, matter, and substances. And you would be surprised at what people will do for money. You'd be equally surprised by the show's popularity. I might find the whole idea utterly ridiculous, and stand amazed that the program lasted as long as it did, but obviously someone was watching it. It would appear that millions of viewers have a lust for the disgusting or they want to see someone else do what they know they could never do in a million years . . . embrace a fear or phobia. While the reasoning and motivation of these contestants may be unimpressive, the ability to not be controlled by fear is an admirable one. And we would do well, as Christians, to overcome our fears . . . because the Word of God tells us, "perfect love casteth out all fear." In the last days, fear of persecution may motivate many to abandon their beliefs and choose the road of temporary safety but permanent destruction. I don't want to be bound by fear. Not that I plan to bungee jump off Seattle's Space Needle or swim any shark tanks anytime soon, but I don't want to be held back by the enemy's grip of fear either. There is most definitely no bed of mice with my name written on it, slippers parked beside it and slumber cap there for me nor is there a worm pit being prepared for Linda in some television studio . . . but Oh to boldly say a word for my Jesus in an uncomfortable setting. To testify of His goodness without fear of repercussion, like the missionaries who risk all to preach the Gospel. That is where trust in God meets chivalry. No doubt, healthy fear is akin to wisdom, but fear that prevents us from realizing the potential God has placed in us is a scary thing. Fear not. Just in case you didn't get it, it's written 48 times in the Old Testament alone, so it must be a point God is trying to drive home. He says, "Fear not, for I am with you." . . . I double dare you to believe Him. Let's pray for the courage to trust in God in the face of our worst fears. His love and power cancel out the fear factor.

Getting What You Want

But when ye pray, use not vain repetitions, as the heathen do: for they think that they shall be heard for their much speaking. ⁸ Be not ye therefore like unto them: for your Father knoweth what things ye have need of, before ye ask him Matthew 6:17-8

Driving down I-5 South on my way home one afternoon, I saw a bumper sticker that made me laugh out loud. It read, "I see. I like. I want. I whine. I get." The sticker was on the rear bumper of a shiny, red sports car driven by an obviously pampered woman. From the looks of things, the slogan was probably true. I was tickled by her open and advertised confession of being spoiled and I must say I wasn't at all mad at her. She had clearly cracked the code for getting what she wanted. Perhaps her methods weren't the best, but who was I to begrudge her. In this world we celebrate ambition and applaud those whom we call "go getters." That bumper sticker versed the sentiment of a society that wants what it wants and will stop at nothing to get it. We are want driven. "I see, I like, I want, I whine, I get." I have used that approach with God from time to time. I'm happy to say it didn't work. Happy because if God had allowed me to get some of the things I craved, they would have ultimately made me miserable. We sometimes plead with God for the things we want and become frustrated when we don't get them. We then set out on our own to get them with disastrous results. The story of David and Bathsheba comes to mind. (2 Samuel, Chapters 11-12) While this woman in the red sports car had apparently found someone to satisfy her every want, who can say if she was truly happy? Getting what we want isn't always what it's cracked up to be. I used to wonder why my mother, who loved God with all her heart, had lived a life of hardship and manual labor and never obtained great wealth.

Certainly she was wealthy in other respects and had things more important than possessions. Yet, I so wanted her to be rich so that she could enjoy luxuries and leisure. In my adult years I tried to provide her with some luxuries but could never give her all the things I wanted her to have. She died never having amassed a fortune. I wondered why God never allowed her to acquire monetary wealth. Then it occurred to me that had she been rich, she might not have depended on God to the extent that she did. Her dependence on Him was a major part of what caused her to love and trust Him so completely. Riches may have stood in the way of that. This led me to the realization that God has not allowed me to have some of the things I've wanted and asked for in this life, because were I to have them I might wind up being lost with them. You see, getting what you want can ultimately cost you everything if what you want isn't what you need. That's right. What we want isn't necessarily what we need. God knows both our wants and our needs and is more concerned about providing for our needs. *But my God shall supply all your need according to His riches in glory by Christ Jesus. (Phil 4:1)* God doesn't pay attention to whining, but He does pay attention to our needs. And He often gives us some of the things we want as well, when those wants are in line with His will and for our good. Ask God to give you the desires of your heart in every sense. This means asking Him to place in us the right desires as well as asking Him to provide for us the things we desire. He has the power to do both.

He Thinks the World of You

In this was manifested the love of God toward us, because that God sent his only begotten Son into the world, that we might live through him. 1 John 4:9

When we contemplate the value that God has placed on each of us, not one Christian should suffer from low self-esteem. I know it's much easier to accept in theory than in reality, but think about it. God loves us so much that He upset all of heaven to redeem us. Knowing everything about us, knowing all of our quirks and flaws, He still thought enough of us to send His Son down here to buy us back from slavery to sin, sacrificing himself for us. Seldom do we really ponder on that. That type of incredible love is hard to fathom. But it's real and you and I are the objects of His incredible affection. Sadly, we forget that at times and fall victim to Satan's attempts to make us feel worthless and disgusting. I once heard a woman pastor petitioning God at a local Prayer Conference. In her public prayer she said, "Jesus, I feel so ugly." She uttered what many of us feel. The harsh effects of sin, combined with the enemy's propaganda, make for a loathsome opinion of ourselves. He'll also use other individuals to assist him in the brainwashing to make us feel unwanted. We may even give in to self-hate. The criticism of self and rehearsing of how terrible we are begins to drown out the loving words of affirmation whispered to us by the One who thought so much of us that He gave His life for ours. We do the devil's job for him. He can now move on to some other evil occupation because we have taken up the task of belittling ourselves. If we would begin to remind ourselves of Whose and who we are, the self-worth issues would dissipate. Having experienced self-doubt, I feel most qualified to write this. In fact, a dear friend once commented to me, while we were having a conversation about my perceived status as a loser, that he would never let anyone speak negatively about me, *including* me. We then began to talk about just how much the Father loves us and how much He has invested in us. The whole world was made for us as a gift of love. That should tell us something about how precious we are to Him. However, for those still questioning how wonderful you are, let me remind you (while I remind myself) of a few things, which I hope will remove any doubt you may have about your worth. First, you are a marvelous creation . . . Psalms 139:14. Someone very important loved you so much that He actually died for you . . . John 3:16. You are a replica of the Almighty . . . Genesis 1:27. You are high priced . . . 1 Corinthians 6:20. He rejoices over you . . . Isaiah 62:5. He has written us so many love letters that there should be no question of how deeply He loves us. When people make us feel small and insignificant, we should keep in mind that God has made a demonstration of just how significant we are to Him by telling us that we are literally "to die for." And He's made an invitation for us to live with Him forever. If that doesn't boost your self-esteem, you may need a ladder.

The Beauty of a Mistake

He hath made everything beautiful in His time.

Ecclesiastes 3:11

The little girl had a harp. She was nine years old and among her many talents was the ability to play this harp. Her name was Rachel. On this particular day, I had just completed worship with the children at the small school. As I left the building, exiting through the classroom, there she sat on the floor in front of her harp. Her mother had allowed her to bring it to school as a sort of "show and tell." I couldn't resist the opportunity to hear her perform, but I wasn't expecting what I would witness. With the grace of an accomplished, adult musician, this petite third grader, with a blond bob and little girl features, began to pluck the strings. The melodies that filled the room were reminiscent of an ancient fairytale. The classroom was transformed into a castle, and she played as if for kings and queens. She completed one song and those of us graced by her gift begged for another. With an apology that she didn't quite recall how to play the next tune, she began tentatively. With each stroke and strum, her confidence grew. The music was soothing and heartwarming. I stood amazed at the gift that had been placed in these small hands. Finally, her mother encouraged her to, "play the song you made up, Rachel." She agreed, with a broad grin, and began plucking a lovely, happy tune. It was an intricate piece that rang joyfully with glad chords and cheerful notes. The melody was inspiring. She smiled as she played and when it was over, she raised her hands above the harp like a dancer. We applauded. This finale was moving. How could a little girl of only nine years have composed such a beautiful and complicated song? Her teacher, asked, "Rachel, how do you write a song like that?" Her response, like her song, went straight from my ears to my heart. "Usually I make a mistake . . . and then I just build on it." This child evangelist had just ministered to me. She said this beautiful song that she had written started with a mistake she made while attempting to play. She then just added to the melody, creating a wonderful song. And it all started with a mistake. What she was essentially telling us was that even a mistake can be turned into something beautiful. A mistake doesn't have to end on a sour note, but it can be rearranged to become an inspiring ballad, a melodious masterpiece, a spirited sonata. And there you have it . . . the beauty of a mistake. Many might say that when God created us and we went astray that we became His biggest mistake. The truth of the matter is that while we might make mistakes, God never does. And by His grace, He can turn even our most discordant mistakes into melodies worthy of praise. All we have to do is take the mistakes and let Him build on them to rearrange the song. Thank you, Rachel.

I Sing Because...

By the rivers of Babylon, there we sat down, yea, we wept, when we remembered Zion. We hange3d our harps upon the willows . . . For there they that carried us away captive required of us a song; and they that wasted us required of us mirth, saying, Sing us one of the songs of Zion. How shall we sing the Lord's song in a strange land? Psalm 137:1-4

The obvious ending to the thought expressed in today's title would be, "I'm Happy." But such isn't always the case in our lives. Yet, we would all benefit from making earnest effort to sing despite circumstances and sing in every situation. Why? Singing has incredible benefits. In this account, the Children of Israel found themselves in captivity again. This time they were the slaves of Babylon and their abductors required of them a song. Certainly this wasn't a situation in which they would most likely feel like singing but they really had no choice in the matter. They had hung up their harps and were exchanging "Woe is me," "Oy Vey" stories, and they asked the rhetorical question, how can we sing when we're in this strange land? I'm sure in your dark and changing times you may have posed the same question. I know I have. How am I supposed to sing at a time like this? My mother's funeral comes to mind. More recently, the sickness and loss of my precious sister Sylvia hangs heavy on my heart. During these and other times, I have been so deep in the recesses of depression and grief, that singing was the last thing on my mind. Facing loss and pain, if I did sing, it would likely have been a downtrodden, slave tune, like Swing Low, Sweet Chariot. But the American slaves found reason to sing, and theirs is an experience, which should inspire us to do likewise. They sang of the hope of things to come. Yes, their songs were a means of

187

communicating with each other and to encourage themselves in their harsh existence, but also a means of speaking to the God Who they trusted would one day deliver them. My mother used to sing while working in a hot nursing home kitchen. My dad whistled while working in steel mills. I wondered how they did it, but later came to realize that they weren't singing about their problems, but singing through them. Their songs were steeped in hope and faith. And, yes, the ability to sing in the midst of adversity is a show of faith. Faith that God will bring you through. Faith that God has not forgotten you and is plotting out your deliverance. So how can you sing? By not getting trapped in the "nowness" of your situation. Yes, I just created a word. Don't look at the problem but look at the outcome. And guess what, singing also has physical benefits. Researchers have linked singing with a lowered heart rate and discovered that singing lowers blood pressure and lessens pain. It even reduces stress. It is believed that singing seems to block the neural pathways that pain travels through. And, singing from the diaphragm increases the blood flow in the body, carrying oxygen and promoting a healthy lymphatic system. This, in turn, increases your immunity. If your children complain about your singing, tell them your trying to fight the flu. Keeping a song in your heart heals the spirit and keeping a song on your lips can help heal the body. And the spiritual benefits are much like the physical. Less depression, less stress, and a healthy heart. Ultimately, your willingness to sing, despite the circumstances, offers God that which He deserves . . . your praise. And praise can unleash miracles in your life, giving you all the more reason to sing. Don't allow the enemy to steal your song. It is your bridge of faith over which to travel from hopelessness to hopefulness, from grief to gratitude, from pain to praise, from darkness to day. *Ye shall have a song, as in the night when holy solemnity is kept; and gladness of heart. Isaiah 30:29*

Losers, Weepers?

I count all things but loss for the excellency of the knowledge of Christ Jesus my Lord: for whom I have suffered the loss of all things, and do count them but dung, that I may win Christ.

Philippians 3:8

As the saying goes, "Finders, keepers; losers, weepers." It denotes the idea that the person who finds something and gets to keep it is better off than the person who's on the losing end. The latter winds up lamenting the fact that he or she lost something that perhaps the first person happily found. This may be plausible in certain instances, but I can think of more than one in which the loser is actually better off. For example the type of loss Paul points to in the text above. He has every reason to be proud of who he is, by the worldly standards of his time and culture. Yet he equates everything that he has gained to nothing, instead rejoicing in the loss he has suffered that allowed him to become better acquainted with God. Some loss indeed draws us nearer to the One who can ease our pain associated with losing. And other types of loss could be considered gain, as well. There are times in life when we lose something that is to our detriment and not in our best interest. This could be a person who mistreats us, or a job that was tearing apart our life or family. In these situations, the particular loss may open the way for the real blessing that God intended for us. God often employs loss as the conduit for gain. And while loss doesn't exactly feel great, if we could adjust our way of thinking for a moment or look at the situation from a different perspective, we might see how some losses could be for our ultimate good. Not all losses, but some. In 1999 the company where I worked closed and I lost my job. The loss prompted me to relocate to a place where I found a better job, met new friends, grew closer to old friends and acquired several things that I had been unsuccessful in acquiring prior to the relocation. While I still mourn the end of that radio ministry, I must also be thankful for that loss. Without it, I might not have experienced the blessings that God had in mind for me at that time. Recognizing the difference between bad and good loss starts by praying this prayer, "Thy will be done." When we align our will with that of God, we can accept certain losses without hopeless despair and discern when loss is an open door. And like Job we can say, "The Lord gave and the Lord hath taken away; blessed be the name of the Lord." When God allows you to lose something, even something precious, trust that He has a purpose for allowing the loss and start looking for the replacement blessing. We tend to try to hold onto things and fight ferociously to avoid losing. Much of it may stem from fear of failure or the unknown. But if we dare to trust God enough to fill the void left by whatever loss we have experienced, we might be surprised by His way of compensating us for the loss. When faced with a painful loss, I remind myself that Samson didn't gain his insight until he lost his eyesight. And let's not forget the type of loss Paul points to in the above passage. All of the great gains he has made he equates to nothing, instead celebrating the suffering that gives him fellowship with Christ. Compensation comes in many forms. It could be something far better than what we lost . . . or maybe it just might turn out to be that closer walk with God derived from the experience. If losing anything allows me to gain an ever-deepening relationship with Christ, stamp "Loser" across my forehead and watch me rejoice. The loser that gains Christ should definitely not be a weeper. I'd say a temporary loss is well worth an eternal gain. *"That I may know him, and the power of his resurrection, and the fellowship of his sufferings, being made conformable unto his death; If by any means I might attain unto the resurrection of the dead." Philippians 3:10-11*

Medicine

It is good for me that I have been afflicted; that I might learn thy statutes. Psalms 119:71

Residents of New England experience some very cold winters. My mother, being what you might call, "old school" believed there was a connection between the cold and colds. So each winter she would purchase Cod Liver Oil, Castor Oil or . . . and I'm dating myself with this one, something called Father John's. She would give each of us a (not so) healthy dose, followed by a slice of orange, to prevent us from catching colds or the flu. It must have worked because I scarcely recall being sick. Sometimes I think the horrible taste of these medicines frightened off whatever sickness might have been lurking. Sure her medical knowledge may not have been taken from the most prestigious medical journals, but her method wasn't too far off. She was attempting to give us preventive medicine. And, preventive medicine is a noble thing. She gave us that disgusting, foul tasting medicine, which by itself seemed like enough to kill us, in hopes of keeping us from experiencing something worse than bad taste. We gagged and wretched and forced it down because our mother told us to, but also because we didn't want to get sick. The terrible medicine served a worthwhile purpose. Sure, it tasted awful, but it was good for us. And so is the medicine that God gives us. It sometimes comes in the form of discomfort or pain. No, He doesn't willfully afflict, but He allows some affliction as a type of preventive medicine . . . to keep us from suffering something worse. We may have to choke it down, but we should be thankful for it. One form of hurt or heartache can often spare us a worse hurt or prevent us from making a terrible mistake that would be far more detrimental. In Psalm 119, David is speaking of the value of the pain he has experienced because it taught him a greater lesson. In other words, the pain was medicine. There have been times in my life when bad experiences that I have endured were later revealed to be a lesser affliction than what would have occurred had it not been for that experience. A broken heart was the medicine that prevented me from entering a relationship with the wrong person. A healthy dose of embarrassment prevented me from making a bigger fool of myself by continuing on a not so smart course. If it hadn't been for the pain, I might have really messed up. One loss prevented me from suffering a greater one. During the intercessory prayer I once offered in church, I thanked God for everything that He allows in our lives, trusting that if He allowed it, then it can only be for our good. I thanked Him for the sorrows that made us lean on Him, the pain that increased our faith, and the trials that made us stronger. After my prayer, a colleague and former fellow classmate of mine gave what he felt was a proper addendum to my prayer. During his sermon he subtly rebuked me saying, "We don't thank God FOR everything, but IN everything we give thanks." Obviously he thought I needed correction. I was well aware of I Thessalonians 5:18, which says, "In everything give thanks for this is the will of God in Christ Jesus concerning you." But in my prayer I had said exactly what I meant. I do thank God for everything because I trust Him just that much. I fully believe that had it not been for some of the suffering and grief I have survived, I might not have survived the greater fall. The afflictions we sometimes face are a form of preventive medicine that inoculates us against the deadlier form of illness. Like the flu shot which gives you a medicinal dose of the illness to help your body ward off the life threatening, full-blown form of Influenza. It was good for me that I was afflicted so that I could learn from it and live through it. The woman you planned to spend the rest of your life with forsook you, thank God for the medicine because she's on husband number 6 now. When the loan doesn't go through, thank you for the medicine, God, because maybe you knew I wouldn't be able to afford it and would have wound up in foreclosure. The boyfriend jilted you, thank you God because perhaps you would have married him and found him to be abusive. You didn't get the well-paying job you applied for at Enron . . . well, you know the rest of that one. Whatever the horrible tasting affliction . . . praise God for the preventive medicine. Romans 8:28 assures us that all things work together for good to them that love God and to those who are the called according to His purpose. Get a slice of orange and open wide. *Psalms 119:67—Before I was afflicted I went astray: but now have I kept thy word.*

Never Too Far

For the Son of Man came to seek and to save what was lost. Luke 19:10

My dear friend's son left his college on a Thursday afternoon to embark upon a 10-hour trip to southern Texas for the wedding of one of his friends. As the caravan made its way across Texas, the car in which he was riding began to overheat and eventually broke down three hours from their destination. And did I mention that one of the passengers in this caravan was the bride? For obvious reasons, failing to make it to the wedding was not an option. So the group called the bride's father and he immediately got in his car and drove the three hours to pick them up and drove them back, saving the day like any Daddy/Hero would. This loving father drove six hours in one day in order to rescue his daughter. It didn't hit me until I was praying with my friend one morning and heard myself say, "Father, you have gone so far to save me." And He really has. Isaiah writes that the ear of God is not so heavy that it cannot hear nor his hand so short that it cannot save but our iniquities have placed us far from Him and now He will not hear us. So we sometimes place ourselves at quite a distance from God. Yet, if we call on Him in our crisis, because He is a loving Daddy/Hero, He will go the distance to save us. I have wandered so far from Him at different points in my life. I've gone so far I had no clue where I was or how to get back. I was, in more than one sense, lost. And I had no one to call on but Him . . . my Father. Just like the father of the bride, He won't leave us broken down on the side of the highway of life. We are never too far away for His love to reach us. I can imagine how relieved and thankful that young bride must have been to see her dad arrive to take her home. I know how relieved and thankful I'll be when my heavenly Father arrives to take me home. I'm sure you feel the same. While we wait for that expected hour, know that regardless of how far you think you've gone, God's love is far reaching. It stretches a whole lot farther than the span of three states. Wherever you are, He is willing to go that distance to reach you. Call on Him. By the way, I'm told the wedding went off without a hitch and was very lovely.

Row by Row

Take therefore no thought for the morrow: for the morrow shall take thought for the things of itself. Sufficient unto the day is the evil thereof. Matthew 6:34

In his youth, my father did a lot of farm work. He picked everything from oranges to beans and everything in between. It was backbreaking, manual labor and sometimes required him to work in record degree heat. I once asked him how he handled such a huge and hard task and he shared with me his strategy. It was more the strength of the mind than the body. He told me that if he looked at the whole field, it was overwhelming and seemed impossible. So he just looked at the row he was working on. He said his goal was just to make it to the end of that row. When he finished it, he would do the same with the next row and the one after that. But this allowed him to harvest large areas of crops without giving up, simply because he set his mind to doing it one row at a time. We heap sorrows upon ourselves at times because we consider everything that can possibly go wrong, we anticipate the worst, and we become consumed with the full weight of a problem. And many times the thing that we were most worried about never happens. It is impossible to deal with every problem that will come your way in life, in advance. Yet, we put ourselves through just as much grief worrying about something as we would actually experience if the thing actually happened. My father's exercise is a brilliant way to handle life's overwhelming situations. Deal with the matter at hand and then move on to the next issue when and if it occurs. Pray and ask God to help you get to the end of that particular row. We will make it through life one experience at a time. If you try to figure out how you're going to handle every possible experience, it will be too overwhelming and seem insurmountable. You may even be inclined to give up. I nearly made myself sick once thinking about how I was going to handle my daughter's teenage years and dating. She was two at the time. I then realized that I'd just have to cross that bridge when I got to it and God would help me. Here's a biblical tip to help you calm down and deal with life one row at a time. *Be anxious for nothing; but in everything by prayer and supplication with thanksgiving let your requests be made known unto God. And the peace of God, which passeth all understanding, shall guard your hearts and minds through Christ Jesus. Philippians 4:6-7* God has already seen your end from the beginning and has a way of helping you through what may even prove to be your worst crisis. You needn't worry about things to come. Let Him get you to the end of each day. As singer/songwriter Cristy Lane so eloquently put it, "One day at a time, sweet Jesus, that's all I'm asking from you. Just give me the strength to do everyday what I have to do. Yesterday's gone, sweet Jesus, and tomorrow may never be mine. Lord help me today, show me the way one day at a time." In my opinion, that's a good prayer and one that each of us would be wise to pray. Give us the strength, Lord, one day . . . or one row, at a time.

So There

There is therefore now no condemnation to them which are in Christ Jesus, who walk not after the flesh, but after the Spirit. Romans 8:1

Guilt is a quirky emotion. In some instances, a person should feel guilty. If you knowingly wrong a person or create a disaster, which you know is definitely your fault, a little guilt can be a good thing. But remorse is a better emotion. Remorse is guilt with change attached to it. Yet, guilt can sometimes be a very destructive emotion. Especially when a person has been forgiven of the wrong and sought to live a changed life. Lingering guilt, in such cases, is made possible courtesy of a grant by the devil, its proud sponsor. Because healthy guilt can bring about changed behavior and repentance, the devil has laid claim to it to use it to get us so bogged down in regret that we discount God's willingness and power to forgive. We spend more time thinking about the wrongful actions and lambasting ourselves over the mistakes. We have no time to focus on the element of forgiveness. God has honored his promise to cast our sins into the deepest part of the sea and we are standing in line at the local sports shop waiting to buy scuba diving equipment. Even when God has let it go, we can't. And sometimes it's because people won't let us. People and things can serve as constant reminders of the goofs we've made, even when we are genuinely remorseful, have repented and been forgiven. This is where the devil's guilt trip recruits passengers. Determine that you will not take the ride. You have dealt with the issue, asked for God to cleanse and forgive, you have changed your ways, and with that you must let go of the guilt. This type of guilt will only hold you back and keep you deeply planted in the mire of regret and shame. Jesus said, "I come not to condemn the world, but so that through me the world might have . . . ." Accept this wonderful pardon and live like it. You can tell the devil and all of his employees you are forgiven, and there is no more condemnation . . . "So There!"

Un-Hatched

And not only so, but we glory in tribulations also: knowing that tribulation worketh patience; And patience, experience; and experience, hope: [5]And hope maketh not ashamed; because the love of God is shed abroad in our hearts by the Holy Ghost which is given unto us. Romans 5:3-5

Cockatiels are supposed to live for about 30 years. Mine did not. I suspect she died from a broken heart. For about 5 years, our home was alive with the delightful chirping sounds and colorful presence of that yellow cockatiel, named Christian. The beautiful bird was a gift from a kind woman whom I met at a women's day event at which I spoke. She raised cockatiels and gave to me the hand-fed little darling, when the bird was only weeks old. I loved that bird. And for the first several years that I had "him" I thought he was a male. That is until one day when I came home to discover three tiny eggs in the bottom of the bird's cage. He was a she! And she had laid eggs as proof. Because she lived alone in her cage, I was at first stupefied as to how she could have laid eggs. After a bit of research and speaking with the breeder, I learned that various changes in a cockatiel's surroundings, and stimulation of sorts can propel female birds into mating mode, even without a mate. I won't go into the graphic details of Christian's private affairs, this is a G rated, family book after all, but suffice it to say she felt the urge to lay eggs . . . to produce. This went on for about 3 days until there were 8 in total. No male in sight, these eggs, of course, were unfertilized. Nevertheless, this dutiful mother hen, I guess you could call her, began sitting on these eggs immediately. She tore the newspaper in her cage into shreds and made a nest, and there she sat on those eggs virtually around the clock. Day after day, there she sat, perched on her hoped for children. She worked diligently to keep the eggs tucked safe and warm underneath her puffed feathers. When one egg would roll out from beneath her, she would scoop it back in, only to have another one of the eight roll out. She would then swiftly stretch her wing to tuck that one back in and so went the scoop, roll, and tuck exercise until she had all 8 nestled precariously beneath her. And there she sat on what I knew to be empty hopes. Never having been fertilized, there was no chance of them ever hatching. One week became two and then three. It was heartbreaking to watch this little creature spending her time and her hopes on eggs that would never produce anything. After the third week, she finally pulled a piece of paper in the bottom of her cage over the eggs, covering them. She seemed to have come to some realization that she was sitting on empty hopes. I eventually took the eggs out of her cage, but she was never the same. She chirped less. She was listless. She wouldn't come out of the cage. And a few months later, she attempted to lay more eggs. But being depleted from the last experience, this new effort to produce claimed her life. The instinct to give birth to something had driven her to try again, even at the risk of fatal consequences. I cannot tell you how I mourned for that bird. She had hope . . . but in vain. It was devastating for me. Certainly because I lost a precious pet, but also because I felt well acquainted with her experience. I knew what it was like to sit on empty hopes. Maybe you do too. Nurturing something you hope will materialize, spending time, emotion, effort, and maybe even money on it only to see it tragically come to naught. It may have been a relationship in which you invested years. Or maybe it was a business plan on which you spent your life savings. An idea? A lifelong ambition? To you I say do not despair. So you dared to hope and it failed to produce. Dare to hope again, first placing your hope in God. My little bird only had half of what it takes to see hope materialize, still she patiently waited for it. You have the hope of being fruitful because of God's involvement. And when you dare to mingle your hopes with God's plan, that's the fertilizer. He'll make what otherwise seems like a goose egg hatch into a joyous accomplishment, far greater than your finite thoughts, even on the strongest hallucinogenic, could have imagined. Dare to allow God to fertilize your dreams and ambitions. Then wait. You see even the germinated outcome that God has in mind may take time to mature. Wait. When God has placed His Holy Spirit power into your deposit, the yield will be fruitful . . . and multiply.

The Ordinance of Humiliation?

Death and life are in the power of the tongue. Proverbs 18:21

Most of us use words everyday, yet we sometimes do not understand the power of them. Words can de-escalate a volatile situation. They can also incite chaos. Words can soothe. They can also scar. It is imperative that we carefully choose our words and fully consider the way they will make others feel. This is especially true of Christians. I once attended a communion service at a local church. I hadn't been to this particular church in quite some time and was thrilled to see many of the people who I hadn't seen in a while. When it was time for the Ordinance of Humility, also known as the foot washing service, I went downstairs in the church and headed into the room where all of the women were assembled and singing hymns as they washed one another's feet. Just as I stepped inside the doorway, a woman greeted me with a big smile and loudly stated, "My goodness, Linda, you're getting FAT!" Just then it felt as if all eyes shifted to me, the singing stopped and everyone began assessing whether this woman's observation was correct. I was suddenly under a spotlight, standing on a large scale with its weight meter hovering over my head in large, illuminated numbers. Of course none of this was the case, but it certainly felt that way. Though shocked, I managed to respond with a cheerful, "It's good to see you too." I embraced this woman and made my way to a chair where my best friend and I could serve one another in this ceremony. When I told my friend what had been said to me, she hugged me and peered at the woman with a death stare. The woman, now chatting happily with others didn't even notice the death rays beaming at her from across the room. It was just as well, because we honestly didn't want her to know how she had injured me with her words, nor did we really wish her any harm. I remember little else of that communion service. The cutting words that had been lobbed at me left me feeling empty and wounded. Did she think for one moment that I didn't realize that I had put on weight? My aching feet and snug fitting clothing had already made the announcement. She had no idea what I may have been going through in my life that induced my weight gain. There was no way for her to know whether I was struggling with it or not. But her words only added to the emotional soup on which I had been dining to my physical demise. Words can help or hinder. Words can cheer or choke. What do the words that you use do for the hearer? Are your words comforting and encouraging or hurtful and crushing? Before you allow them to leave your lips, hear them for yourself and decide whether these are words that you would like to hear uttered to you. Let no corrupt communication proceed from your mouth. There is life and death in the tongue. Are you speaking living words or are your words deadly?

The Sting of Death

Then when lust hath conceived, it bringeth forth sin: and sin, when it is finished, bringeth forth death. James 1:15

The caption read, "Deadly Sting." News reports announced that Crocodile Hunter Steve Irwin was dead. Irwin had been killed by a stingray, ironically, while taping a segment for a children's program, and not even one of his more daring shows. In fact, at the time of his death, he was taking a break from filming a show called, "The Ocean's Deadliest" in order to film the documentary for children. To many, although tragic and sad, Irwin's death came as no surprise. The 36-year old naturalist had spent his life trying to make crocodiles, snakes, and sharks appear more loveable. The Aussie croc hunter became famous for his fearless approach to creatures from which most would flee. Stingrays can attack when provoked or stressed. Experts say a stingray's attack is rarely deadly, but is always painful. A stingray's barb at the end of its tail is serrated like a knife and covered with a thin layer of tissue, which contains venom. As Irwin and his underwater cameraman swam near the Barrier Reef off Port Douglas in Australia, Irwin came dangerously close to a massive stingray. Its barb punctured Irwin's chest and heart and he died within minutes. It was said that he died doing what he loved. Certainly that didn't make his untimely death anymore worthwhile. When I heard the report, I couldn't help but see the spiritual correlation. It sounded a lot like how dangerously close we come to sin . . . and even Satan. Like Irwin, we begin to feel invincible because the attacks of Satan have not proved fatal . . . yet. We fearlessly go into the dark recesses where sin exists and toy with the devil on his territory. Unlike Irwin, we may not have turned our passion into primetime entertainment, nor have we become famous for our thrill-seeking stunts. However, the same outcome may await us if we persist in satisfying this fascination with what we know can be harmful to us. Although we may not necessarily seek it out, we flirt with danger and sin, and even enjoy the excitement of it. And when we least expect it, the devil will eventually attack us and puncture us with his venomous weapon. God wants to protect us from this attack, but we have to safeguard ourselves against it as well. Today's text gives a warning of the inevitable outcome of giving in to our wanton desires and pleasure seeking. Death. We can take steps to avoid this outcome. First, stay out of the devil's territory. Poet Alexander Pope once said "Fools rush in where angels fear to tread." Avoid temptation. Then, put on the whole armor of God. (Ephesians 6) This is an effective shield against the wiles of the devil, if we wear it. When we willingly and eagerly walk into the devil's playground and attempt to wrestle with him like a crocodile, we risk death. When we do all we can to resist the devil and his temptations, God offers us power to overcome. *Behold, I give unto you power to tread on serpents and scorpions, and over all the power of the enemy: and nothing shall by any means hurt you (Luke 10:19).*

Who Knew? Answer: God

[15]My substance was not hid from thee, when I was made in secret, and curiously wrought in the lowest parts of the earth.[16]Thine eyes did see my substance, yet being unperfect; and in thy book all my members were written, which in continuance were fashioned, when as yet there was none of them. Psalm 139:15-16

I was sitting in the funeral service of a young man who suffered what I believed to be an untimely death at the age of 50. As I looked at the grey coffin, blanketed with a white spray of flowers, I rehearsed the end. This man's life was over. Had he accomplished all that he had planned and aspired to do? Was his life complete? I couldn't help but reflect on my own life and ask the same questions. Had I . . . ? In the days leading up to this end event, I had been asking those very questions and was not particularly happy about the answers I gave myself. One of the pastors stood to read from the Old and then New Testaments, as is typically done at funerals. I didn't hear the New Testament reading because I was fixed on the Old Testament text.

Whither shall I go from thy spirit? Or whither shall I flee from thy presence? If I ascend up into heaven, thou art there: if I make my bed in hell, behold, thou art there. If I take the wings of the morning, and dwell in the uttermost parts of the sea; Even there shall thy hand lead me, and thy right hand shall hold me. If I say, Surely the darkness shall cover me; even the night shall be light about me. Yea, the darkness hideth not from thee; but the night shineth as the day: the darkness and the light are both alike to thee. For thou hast possessed my reins: thou hast covered me in my mother's womb. I will praise thee; for I am fearfully and wonderfully made: Marvelous are thy works; and that my soul knoweth right well. My substance was not hid from thee, when I was made in secret, and curiously wrought in the lowest parts of the earth. Thine eyes did see my substance, yet being unperfect; and in thy book all my members were written, which in continuance were fashioned, when as yet there was none of them. How precious also are thy thoughts unto me, O God! How great is the sum of them!

Who knew this man would die? Who knew his children would be left to live their lives without a father to counsel and encourage them? Who knew I would suffer the losses in my life that could not be prevented? Who knew I would make bad choices and make mistakes and lose my mother and wind up divorced? Who knew? Then the answer was contained in the lengthy text above. It basically says, God knew. Even before I was born, God knew me. His eyes saw my substance before I was formed. He knew what I would face. He knew what I would become. And no matter where I find myself, the God who knew me would be there with me. Who knew this young man would reach this end? God knew. He made him . . . fearfully and wonderfully, despite the cancer. Did this young man accomplish everything he planned? Maybe not, but God knew and made plans for the young man Himself. So we may go through dark times of doubt, but even the night will shine like daytime. We have no reason to fear the unknown, because nothing is unknown to God. And since He knew us before we were born, I'm pretty sure He has us covered right up to the close of this life He gave us. In that we can have peace. As those who knew this young man spoke of him, it was clear that He trusted God even in his final and painful days. He trusted that God knew what was best for him in his life. That type of trust only comes from believing that God cares. And He definitely does. So much so, in fact, that before we were even breathed into existence, He saw the outline of our form and future. Then to confirm the fact that He cares, for those times when the unforeseen, like death or illness, may force their way into our existence, He offered these words, Casting all your cares upon Him for he CARETH for you. Should you begin to wonder about the why of what you are going through or the unexpected nature of your difficulties, when that puzzling feeling gives way to the question, "who knew?" remember God did . . . and He cared enough to make even the worst turn out all right, ultimately.

Life Stages

He hath made every thing beautiful in his time: Ecclesiastes 3:11

It was summer and life had been so fast paced that quite a bit had passed me by. Funny how living sometimes controls the speed of life. So in an effort to slow things down and regain control, I got up early that Sunday morning and decided to go for a walk. While on my favorite trail, I realized that one of the things that had passed me by was the blooming and blossoming of the blackberry bushes along the way. I stopped to take a closer look . . . okay, and to eat a few (yes, without washing them) and was delighted to see how beautifully they were developing. My mind and spirit being wide open on this morning, I also made another observation that I found quite encouraging. There were mature and maturing berries all on the same vine. Some were still green and small, others were large and dark and bursting with sweet juice. And then, there were those that were somewhere in the middle. They were red, their hue giving hope of development. But they were all clustered there together on the same vine. Some having arrived at their peak, others still making their way there. I smiled in my spirit, considering the blessing in that revelation. As I moved on along the trail, I passed a family enjoying a morning outing. We nodded at each other, moving in opposite directions. Reaching the end, I doubled back to make my return walk and eventually I caught up with this family again. There were 5 of them. Mom, Dad, one older boy on a bike, a younger girl on a small pink bike with training wheels, and a smaller boy riding a little scooter. I had caught up with them because they were going up hill, the mom pushing the little ones along. When they reached the top of the hill and started going downhill the children began to pick up speed and I jokingly mentioned to the Mom, "I hope they know how to work the brakes." She laughed and then ran to catch them, grabbing hold of them to slow them down. This continued with each hill until they had gained a considerable distance ahead of me, as the mother ran alongside her children. I stopped again to take pictures at which point the dad, who had lagged behind, passed me by and caught up with his family. When I resumed my walking and completed my iPhotography expedition, I looked ahead and watched this beautiful family. The mom was now carrying the little one's scooter and holding his hand as he walked up hill beside her. A few minutes later she was carrying him AND the scooter. Soon dad placed him on his shoulders as they all walked slowly along the trail together. As I passed them I had to stop and share what watching them had done for me. "Your family has been such an inspiration to me this morning," I said to the woman and her husband. They looked surprised and said, "Thank you! How?" I told them how I had watched as these caring parents had pushed their children along up hill, chased and slowed them down, ran alongside them, and then eventually wound up carrying them. Their faces lit up and huge smiles formed. "Thank you so much," they told me, the Dad commenting, "Sort of like life, huh?" I remarked, "Exactly!" We exchanged more smiles and warm words of mutual appreciation and then I told them I would be sharing their story in my writing. How could I not? God had given me two clear examples of the stages of life and the beauty of each. I'm certain it's because of the place where I am in my own life and God's desire to remind me that it's all good. He allows the mature and the maturing to grow on the same vine. And sometimes there are those who can walk and those who need to be carried all in the same family. Whatever the stage of life, each is important and valuable because growth is present. Somewhere in the process, there will be sweetness. Living slowed down enough that day to allow me to see life.

I Got Shoes

Now when Jesus heard these things, he said unto him, Yet lackest thou one thing: sell all that thou hast, and distribute unto the poor, and thou shalt have treasure in heaven: and come, follow me. Luke 18:22

As I type, a cascade of shoes pouring out of my closet onto my bedroom floor serves as a backdrop for this writing. I have a shoe fetish and must admit that it borders on addiction. With that statement, perhaps I take my first step toward help. If there is a shoe sale, I'm there. If there isn't a shoe sale, I'm there. It's not because I grew up deprived of shoes. My father tells heart-wrenching stories of how as a child of hard times in the Deep South, he rarely had shoes. When he and his siblings did get a pair they would walk to school barefoot and put their shoes on once they arrived to save wear and tear on them. Though sad and depressing, I can't even say that's why I love shoes. I just can't pass up a pair of attractive shoes. My mother was the same, often purchasing the same shoes in different colors. Call it frivolity, she too just had a shoe thing and must have passed along her obsession to me. Even though I'm shoe crazy, I dare say that I have so many pairs that they often become bothersome as I dig through disorganized piles of them looking for the right pair. This alerts me to the fact that we can actually have too much of a good thing. And that excess, if left unchecked, can lessen our appreciation for things while increasing our obsession with things and giving us a false sense of heaven on earth. The American slaves used to sing a Negro Spiritual, which said, "I got shoes, you got shoes, all God's chillun got shoes. When I get to heaven, gonna put on my shoes and an gonna walk all over God's heaven." How heartbreaking to think that their idea of heaven was that it was merely a place where every one of God's children would have his or her own pair of shoes. But that hope was based on what they lacked. As slaves, the thought of freedom was also their idea of heaven. To the person with bare feet, shoes are a heavenly thought. To the homeless, a place to lay your head is heaven. Whatever the need, having it met is heavenly. And that is what makes heaven so desirous. The idea that our needs will be met there. We should cherish that thought to the point where we are willing to give up anything *here* to get to *there*. The place where our loneliness, sorrow, poverty, sickness, depression, and loss will all be figments of a past that we will scarcely remember. But if we lack little here on earth, will we still desire heaven? I'd hate to get so comfortable with all of my "shoes" that I lose sight of heaven. I'm keenly aware that "things" can cloud our view at times. That may be why the tag line of that Negro Spiritual I spoke about earlier warned, "Everybody talkin' bout heaven ain't goin' there." Because just as real as the hope of heaven may be, the risk of not making it is equally as real if we lose sight of it to "things". Whether we are in a state of lacking or plenty, we should have our focus on heaven and the wonders it will offer. Don't let shoes, or whatever your obsession, get in the way. Things are nice, "but seek ye first the kingdom of God, and his righteousness; and all these things shall be added unto you." (Matthew 6:33) If we let the things that have been added to our lives subtract from the pursuit of heaven, we lose entirely and eternally. As much as I love shoes, I'm looking forward to the day when I'll leave every pair behind. Nothing on this earth is an adequate substitute for what lies in store for us. It's been said that eyes haven't seen nor ears heard the wonderful things that God is preparing for those of us who love Him. I can't wait to see what tops shoes. More importantly, I can't wait to see the One whose shoes I'm not even worthy to carry.

Handheld Pieces of Life

Touch is a powerful thing. This is why I love hands. Through touch, they carry out the desires of the heart. They catch us when we fall, they wipe away tears, they feed us, they hold us, they lift us. We can use our hands to bless others. For me, hands are an emblem of love. The following 12 photographs are reflections of 12 experiences where the touch of a hand connected hearts. When Jesus performed the miracle of feeding the multitude, He used His hands to take the food and bless it . . . it then nourished. There were 12 baskets remaining of the fragments. These photographs are fragments of love . . . these are the leftovers.

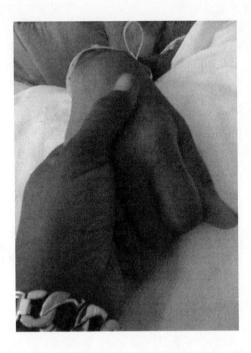

I will always treasure the moment when I held my sister Sylvia's hand during her illness. Our hands, just like our hearts, will forever be connected. The warmth of her touch can still be felt.

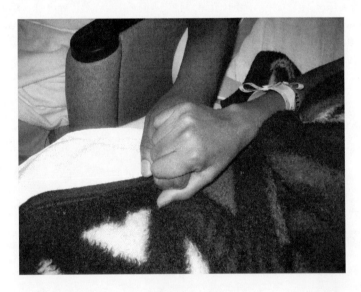

Sylvia holding her husband Woody's hand . . . which she held in marriage for 25 years. He has the fragments.

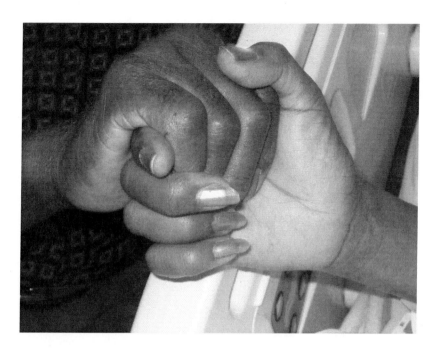

Daddy holding his daughter's hand . . .

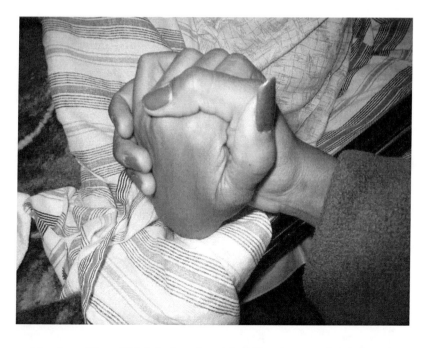

My niece Nina (Sylvia's daughter) holding her mother's hand.

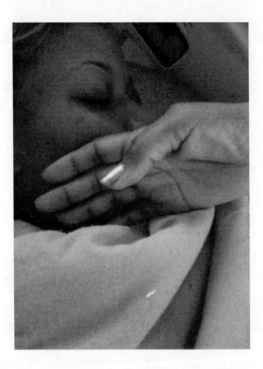

Sylvia touching her daughter's face as she slept. She had asked me to push the folding bed closer to her hospital bed so she could reach her. Though asleep, I hope Nina will always remember that touch.

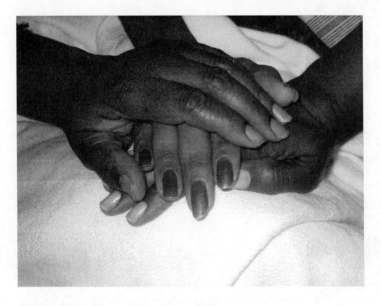

Sisters . . . Marionette, Sylvia and I made a pact of love.

Sylvia's best friend Cassie made this quilt by hand and brought it to her. They held hands. It was their last visit.

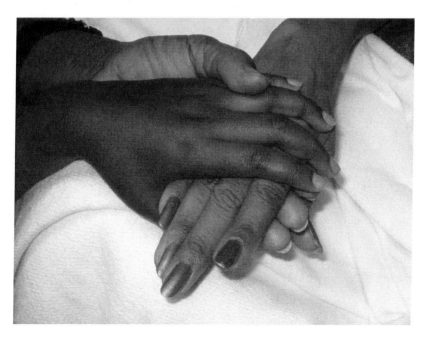

Marionette and her granddaughter Makayla holding hands with Sylvia. They made a memory in that moment.

My brother Gil and his wife made several trips to minister to
Syl. What a special last touch. What a special last fragment.

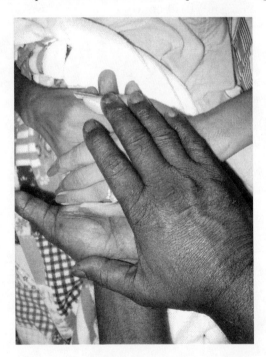

My eldest brother Al, though ill, traveled to see Sylvia one
last time. They held hands as they said farewell.

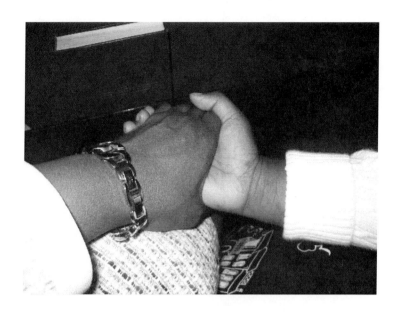

The comfort of holding hands. My great niece
Makayla held mine . . . when we needed it most.

Mother and daughter . . . I pray she never lets go.

"Fragments of Life"

My mother handing gifts to my sister Marionette and me at
Christmas, as my brother Bobby looks on.

The Anderson family just after relocating to Connecticut from Florida in the 1950's. My paternal grandparents migrated also. (Top row, far left.)

Sitting on my mother's lap in front of our Connecticut home.

Nette, Syl, and Lin in Atlanta in 2009, gathering fragments at our Sisters' Weekend in celebration of the 60th birthday of a dear friend.

Hugs are some of the best fragments . . .

Mom and Dad at church in Hartford, CT . . . lots of
memories there.

Celebrating Daddy's 80th Birthday . . .

Daddy and most of his grandchildren. Your children's
children will bless you!

(Top Row: Brandon, Ariel, Brooke, Tameka, Nina, Frederick.
Bottom Row: Marcina, Dad, Jacob.
Missing: Skylah, Daphne, Angela, Douglas, Donovan,
Amber, Crystal, Lee, Reuben.)

7 of my parents' 9 children . . .

(Top Row: Lin, Syl, Mike, Julie, Nette.
Bottom Row: Al, Dad, Gil. Missing: Lucy Ann, Bob.)

Daddy's loving hands are still strong enough to hold
even his great grandchildren!

"Photographs courtesy of Jacob Anderson, Gilbert Anderson, Linda Anderson, Elana Haveles-Owens, and Cassandra Mantoni."